Bold Women of Medicine
21 Stories of Astounding Discoveries, Daring Surgeries, and Healing Breakthroughs

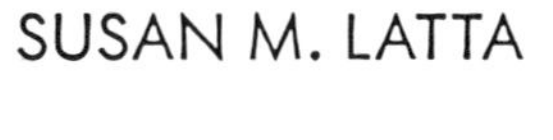
SUSAN M. LATTA

CHICAGO
REVIEW
PRESS

To Rob, Ryan, Kristen, and Robbie: all my love.

Published by Chicago Review Press Incorporated
814 North Franklin Street
Chicago, Illinois 60610
ISBN 978-1-61373-437-7

Library of Congress Cataloging-in-Publication Data

Names: Latta, Susan M.
Title: Bold women of medicine : 21 stories of astounding discoveries, daring surgeries, and healing breakthroughs / Susan M. Latta.
Description: Chicago, Illinois : Chicago Review Press, [2017] | Audience: Age 12+ | Includes bibliographical references and index.
Identifiers: LCCN 2016057949 (print) | LCCN 2016058484 (ebook) | ISBN 9781613734377 (cloth : alk. paper) | ISBN 9781613734384 (pdf) | ISBN 9781613734407 (epub) | ISBN 9781613734391 (Kindle)
Subjects: LCSH: Women in medicine—Biography. | Women in medicine—History. | Women physicians—Biography. | Women physicians—History. | Nurses—Biography. | Nurses—History.
Classification: LCC R692 .L37 2017 (print) | LCC R692 (ebook) | DDC 610.82—dc23
LC record available at https://lccn.loc.gov/2016057949

Interior design: Sarah Olson

Printed in the United States of America
5 4 3 2 1

Contents

PART III: AND TODAY STILL FIGHTING

FOREWORD

Shaped by Experiences

As I think about how I would describe myself today, there are the titles of student, future doctor, wife, daughter, sister, and dog lover, but more than just these labels are the experiences I have had in life that shaped me into who I am today.

I was born into medicine on October 19, 1986, in Rochester, Minnesota, where my mom was working as an orthopedic (dealing with bones and muscles) nurse and my dad was in his first year of an orthopedic surgery residency at the Mayo Clinic. Medicine was unintentionally ingrained into my daily routine. My dad worked long hours as a resident, and often we would go to the hospital to have dinner with him. After his training, we moved to Aberdeen, South Dakota, and this small town became my home.

Medicine continued to be part of my life. I would spend Sunday after church making rounds with my dad at the hospital and during the week would go to the clinic to help him see patients. While at times I was probably more work for my dad's

Gina Routh, National President of the Student Osteopathic Medical Association, 2015, left, holding the sign with representatives and future doctors from Des Moines University. *Courtesy of Gina Routh*

secretary, I enjoyed even the little jobs like putting stickers on charts. I loved being part of medicine.

I watched my first total knee replacement surgery when I was 14 years old. At the time, I thought it was going to be this amazing experience. I was so nervous and excited about being in the operating room I ended up fainting in the hallway during the surgery. I thought for sure my career in medicine was over before it even began. It was an embarrassing experience for a 14-year-old, but it solidified my drive to be a compassionate physician.

My mom also encouraged me to be thankful for the blessings I have in my life, and I witnessed her giving back to the community through numerous volunteer projects all while raising two crazy kids and teaching nursing skills at the local college. She was a true role model.

During high school I continued to immerse myself in many different activities. I volunteered at the hospital and at my church teaching bible study. I was the vice president of the student council, on the prom committee, and captain of the flags team. I even combined my leadership activities with medicine and put together a health fair for my entire high school.

When I started to look for a college, I wanted to find a community that would allow me to discover what I wanted to be in life but would also give me the fun college experience that so many high school seniors want. I found Creighton University in Omaha, Nebraska. I developed friendships that became my family away from home and fell in love with my now husband, Jared.

Because I had been "born into medicine," I wanted to make sure that this was what I really wanted to do with my life—not just something that was expected of me. I volunteered at Creighton Memorial St. Joseph's Hospital on Creighton's campus and began to shadow physicians in different specialties. I majored in exercise science with a minor in biology and continued to be a leader by getting involved in my sorority, Gamma Phi Beta, the Greek Life Honor Society, and other Omaha organizations. One summer I studied abroad in Kunming, China, focusing on traditional Chinese medicine, culture, and language.

When I was ready to apply to medical school, I was terrified and overjoyed all at once. I went through the application and interview process over many months. I was not successful in getting accepted into medical school the first time I applied. My life plan was ruined, or at least I thought it was, when I found out I wasn't going to become a doctor. To say I took the news well would be a lie. I was devastated. I was a "type-A" planner to the core, and this changed everything. However, I was determined to try again.

Jared, my boyfriend at the time, had been accepted to Creighton University for medical school. I began plan B by applying to Creighton for a master's degree in anatomy and physiology, an 18-month program. At about the same time, I was hired to work as an undergraduate admissions counselor at Creighton, which was the complete opposite of what my career goals had been the year prior. I took a break from medicine to get married and was able to spend a year with my husband.

I was still a leader but in a different capacity. I mentored young high school students and walked through the college application process with first-generation college students. After temporarily stepping away from medicine, I was able to refocus my goals about the kind of doctor I wanted to be.

My second round of medical school applications was more successful, and I was accepted into Des Moines University (DMU). In August 2012 I temporarily left my husband and dog

Gina at SOMA conference. *Courtesy of Gina Routh*

behind in Omaha to live in a small apartment and begin learning to be a doctor. I got involved in campus events, and my first year I served as the Student Osteopathic Medical Association (SOMA) First-Year Liaison.

The next year I was the president of the DMU SOMA chapter and was exposed to National SOMA in Chicago, Illinois, during the summer leadership conference. I became the National SOMA Region III Trustee, and this past year I was elected into the position as the National SOMA president. I knew I wanted to be part of SOMA because it is a voice for osteopathic students who are the future of osteopathic medicine.

Healthcare is complex and affects real people, which is why making a difference in the field is so rewarding. It is a business, but it is the business of caring for the human race, which makes changing it so personal. I wanted to be part of the change and influence the decisions that were being made for my patients and colleagues, and SOMA allowed me to do that.

SOMA strives to be a voice and mentor to future doctors. Students can have a direct influence by participating in national discussions. The discussions result in a number of resolutions being passed at the American Osteopathic Association House of Delegates. It is accountable, has a focus on development, and is visible. These are all qualities that make me proud to be the leader to more than 14,000 SOMA members.

Each low point and each challenge has shaped me into the person I am today. Surely more challenges will present themselves on the way to becoming an internal medicine physician, but I hope to continue to be a leader to help make a difference. It was the support of my husband, parents, and brother that reminded me to do the hard things in life. You can be surprised at how amazing you really are!

—Gina Routh, DO

INTRODUCTION

"Go Tomorrow to the Hospital to See the She Doctors!"

Thirty-four female medical students from the Woman's Medical College of Pennsylvania arrived at the Pennsylvania Hospital amphitheater on November 6, 1869. Up until this time, men had had at their disposal laboratories and surgical observation rooms where they could gain valuable clinical experience. Women had books and classroom lectures. Without opportunities for firsthand observation, women did not have a complete medical education.

A deal had been struck with Pennsylvania Hospital. The women were invited to join several hundred male medical students to observe surgeries and labs and hear two clinical lectures on how to treat sick and injured patients.

On November 8, 1869, the *Philadelphia Evening Bulletin* wrote an account of the event that became known as the "mob of '69" or "the jeering episode."

> When the ladies entered the amphitheater they were greeted by yells, hisses, "caterwaulings," mock applause, offensive remarks upon personal appearance., etc. . . . Various rude manifestations were made—missiles of paper, tin-foil, tobacco-quids, etc. were thrown upon the ladies, while some of these *men* (?) defiled the dresses of the ladies near them by spirting tobacco-juice upon them.

Throughout this demonstration, the ladies maintained their quiet poise. They hadn't gotten this far without realizing how important it was to take their scientific studies seriously. At the end of the account, the paper stated, "It is hoped that this narrow-minded policy will have died a natural death before next Saturday, and that each man will remember his own mother or sisters before he joins in insulting women of virtue and intelligence."

Anna Broomall, one of the medical students in attendance that day, recalled the event years later.

> When we turned up at the clinic, in what was then the new amphitheater, pandemonium broke loose: the students rushed in pell-mell, stood up in the seats, hooted, called us names and threw spitballs, trying in vain to dislodge us. . . . When at last the second hour came to an end, as all things must, we had scarcely heard a word of what our preceptors had been trying to tell us. We were hustled and jostled into the hall. . . . Borne along as on the crest of a wave, we found ourselves in 8th Street and went twenty different ways, still pursued by taunts and jeers. The present generation should be given to know what such women have done for all other women. More than one among us hold in her capable hands the lamp of Florence Nightingale, and the flame of it burns bright and clear.

This event occurred almost 21 years after Elizabeth Blackwell had graduated as a physician and about 15 years after Florence Nightingale's astonishing accomplishments during the Crimean War.

Even though medical women faced such obstacles with steely resolve, they were not always confident. They survived many failures on the way to success. They were jeered at, put down, shunned, and not considered intelligent enough for careers in medicine. When "no" was the first answer they received, they searched elsewhere for a "yes." They simply would not be denied.

I wrote out the final list of women for this book on a piece of scratch paper, and to save time I used only their first names. Then it dawned on me. They had become so familiar over the last year that there was no other way to refer to them. Florence, Elizabeth, Clara, Marie, Rebecca, Mary, and so on. Wouldn't it be cool to gather all 21 women and share stories? Our customs and dress would be so different. They would surely be amazed and proud of the barriers they had all broken for women in medicine.

PART I
The Bold Pioneers

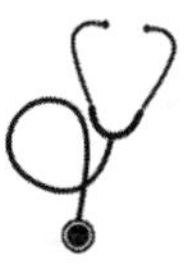

For what is done or learned by one class of women becomes, by virtue of their common womanhood, the property of all women.

—ELIZABETH BLACKWELL

From the beginning of human civilization, women—whether trained or not—have been healers. For centuries they tended to and healed the sick in the home or the private area of life. The bold pioneers of medicine highlighted in this section began to change that. Born within a quarter century of each other, 1820 through 1846, they and other 19th-century medical women bravely left the home to practice medicine more publicly, regardless of what was said about them.

Many of these pioneering medical women did not have formal training but made the transition between private and public practice by providing nutrition and hygiene knowledge to other women and their families. In 1835 self-taught Harriot

Hunt tended to her seriously ill sister using medical practitioners Elizabeth and Richard Mott's system of healing with herbs, roots, and oils. When Harriot's sister recovered, they practiced medicine together, without degrees, and built up a successful business.

Twelve years later, after witnessing the first woman, Elizabeth Blackwell, graduate from medical school in the United States, Harriot Hunt applied to Harvard Medical School. She was rejected twice, though the school allowed her to purchase lecture tickets. Within a few months, however, that opportunity was also terminated, and Harvard did not allow the admission of women until 1946. The Woman's Medical College of Pennsylvania awarded an honorary degree to Harriot in 1854.

The bold pioneers all had parts to play in the American Civil War, or in Florence Nightingale's case, the Crimean War. Women were needed to nurse and comfort the many wounded soldiers. Marie Zakrzewska opened the New England Hospital for Women and Children in July 1862 with the aim of training women to be both physicians and nurses. Trained or not, women crept onto the battlefields, their presence neither approved nor desired. But they proved themselves in their ability to act swiftly and courageously. The massive amount of wounded and sick soldiers created a need that could no longer be met with men alone. Both the Crimean War in Europe and the American Civil War illuminated women's medical capabilities.

Female medical pioneers tackled tasks and jobs that men said they didn't have the brainpower or stamina to do. They studied. They observed surgeries. Sometimes they swooned at the gruesomeness of medicine, but so did the men. Even if they became queasy, wobbled, or fainted, they went back for more. They invented treatments, discovered what worked and what didn't, and set out to heal.

They fought hard, even within their own families, for acceptance. Mary Putnam Jacobi (1842–1906) was one of the pioneering women physicians when she graduated from the Woman's Medical College of Pennsylvania in 1864. Her own father wrote to her upon entrance to the school, "You know very well that I am proud of your abilities [but] . . . be a lady from the dotting of your I's to the color of your ribbons—and if you must be a doctor and philosopher, be an attractive and agreeable one."

Many of these women had a natural love for science and how the body works. They endeavored to ease pain and suffering. They searched for the joy on the faces of women who were handed healthy newborns. They struggled to be part of a battle's action and help the wounded make it home to their loved ones. It was their compassion combined with know-how and a tough stomach that helped them succeed.

Several of the medical pioneers had something in common. They had parents, and especially fathers, who were forward thinking. These parents believed their daughters had as much right to education as their sons. Sometimes, though, even after the parents went to great lengths to educate them, they still believed their daughters should marry and take their place in the home. Learning might damage young women's "delicate" systems or, worse, destroy their femininity. Were they smart enough to enter the medical field? Of course they were—Elizabeth Blackwell finished first in her class—but men didn't think so.

Women such as Clara Barton and Mary Walker were severely criticized for their ambitions and competence. If a woman didn't marry or want to be married, her intentions were suspect. If she looked to the outside world for her identity, wanted higher education and a career, or worked in the company of men, her morals were questioned and her reputation suffered.

By opening these doors in the mid-1800s, Elizabeth Blackwell, Florence Nightingale, and other female medical pioneers made it possible for many women to pursue medical career paths.

Florence Nightingale

Victorian Rule Breaker

I think one's feelings waste themselves in words; they ought all to be distilled into actions, and into actions which bring results.

At the time of Florence Nightingale's birth on May 12, 1820, a new class of people was emerging in Great Britain. Their ancestors had been working class, but this new group purchased larger homes, made friends with influential people, and gained status as high society accepted them. Florence's father, William Shore Nightingale, was a prosperous landowner who had inherited two estates in England. The family traveled, entertained, and did charity work. Real work was out of the question; it would lower their social standing.

The Industrial Revolution brought automated manufacturing to the big cities. Factory workers returned home to slums with impure drinking water and little food. When the poor

Florence Nightingale, circa 1860. *Wikimedia Commons*

got sick, they were carted to hospitals, most often dying there, while the rich were treated at home. Those were the rules of the era. Young Florence was outraged and was determined to change things.

Florence—named after the city Florence, Italy, in which she was born—and her older sister, Parthenope—named after Parthenopolis, a Greek settlement near Naples, Italy—were taught several languages as well as mathematics and philosophy. When Florence turned 12, her father took charge of her and her sister's educations, which was extremely rare.

Florence didn't want to follow tradition by marrying and raising a family. She longed "for something worth doing instead of frittering time away on useless trifles." Her mother didn't understand her habit of daydreaming and believed there was something horribly wrong with her.

A flu epidemic hit the Nightingale household and surrounding village in January 1837, and Florence tended to the sick. Shortly after, on February 7, 1837, she claimed to have heard God calling her. She said, "God spoke to me and called me to His service." She had no idea what God had in store for her.

Florence tried to figure out how she could best help the village people. In 1845 she presented a plan to her parents. She would study nursing at the Salisbury Infirmary under the guidance of a close family friend, Dr. Richard Fowler. Her parents and extended family were horrified by her yearnings. Every time she brought up the subject to her sister or mother, they would swoon and faint, taking to their beds. How could she humiliate them like this?

In a letter to her father, Florence complained about women struggling to put their abilities to use. She said, "Why cannot a woman follow abstractions like a man? Has she less imagination, less intellect, less self-devotion, less religion than a man? I think not. . . . It cuts her wings, it palsies her muscles, and shortens her breath for higher things and for a clearer, but sharper, atmosphere, in which she has no lungs to live. She has fed on sugar plums, her appetite is palled for bread."

Florence had received offers of marriage, one from her first cousin (not unusual for the time) Henry Nicholson and one from Richard Monckton Milnes, who pined after her for years. But she didn't see the point of married life when she could be useful to the sick.

To dampen Florence's nursing desires, her parents allowed her to travel. She traveled with an older couple, Charles and Selena Bracebridge, who introduced her to influential people, the most important of these being Sidney and Elizabeth Herbert. Social reform was one of the Herberts' interests, and they became fast friends with Florence.

At first Florence's travels energized her. She was allowed the freedom of exploration that she had never had before. Then the daydreams that plagued her throughout childhood returned. She was inflicted with headaches and feared she was losing her mind. She languished in her room with scarcely the energy to get out of bed.

Her worried chaperones took her to the Institute for Protestant Deaconesses at Kaiserswerth, Germany, to be examined by a doctor. A few years earlier, she had wanted to study nursing there, but her parents had forbidden the trip. Now she traveled to the institute without permission. When her mother found out, she demanded that Florence return home to help her sister, Parthe, get over her recent illness.

Once again Florence was trapped! But no one could stop her from corresponding with important people on medical and social policy. About a year later, she escorted her ill sister (no one really knew what was wrong with Parthe) back to the Kaiserswerth Institute. This time Florence was finally allowed to attend nurses' training.

Her living arrangements at Kaiserswerth were brutal—waking at 5:00 AM, suffering through hours of instructions only to be rewarded with measly food of thin vegetable broth, rye tea, and black bread. Still, Florence was thrilled to assist at surgeries and ached to lead a bustling public medical facility. The head pastor complimented her to Sidney Herbert, her influential friend back in England, as the most talented nursing intern the institute had yet trained.

Florence, now nearly 35, was still seeking permission from her parents to do as she wished! But when Liz Herbert proposed Florence as the new superintendent for the Harley Street Home, a small charity hospital for poor women, Florence jumped at the chance, ignoring her mother's protests. It wasn't considered ladylike at that time to be paid by an employer, so Florence's father stepped in and offered her an allowance of £500 per year—today about $57,000 per year.

Florence worked diligently and within just a few months had transformed the hospital from an inefficient charity hospital into a place of well-being. She ordered new equipment, trained nurses, and kept a careful inventory of supplies. The hospital's efficiency had improved so much that Florence began to look for a new challenge.

Most nurses in the 1850s were uneducated. They were considered to have come from the lower class and of no higher social status than prostitutes. Their pay was next to nothing, and many drank as they worked. The profession was in dire need of an overhaul, and Florence was up to the task. But Russia's unwanted expansion plans thwarted her wish to establish a nursing school.

In March 1854, as Russia forged into Turkey seeking Constantinople's Black Sea port, England and France joined forces with Turkey, entering the Crimean War. Britain's valuable trade routes had to be protected. But the British Army's inept officers and careless and often incomplete paperwork caused chaos as thousands of unprepared men were shipped off to the Crimean Peninsula to fight.

The soldiers who weren't killed by Russian gunfire soon became ill with cholera and other diseases. The wounded and sick were piled onto overcrowded, undersupplied ships bound for an old barracks in Scutari, Turkey. Supplies had been ordered but were slow to appear.

With no food, no bedding, not even a cup for a desperately needed drink of water, the soldiers suffered. The barracks had been built over cesspools. Sewer lines were often blocked, leading to overflow throughout the hallways, which in turn contaminated most of the water supply.

When reports of the soldiers' plight reached England, Florence jumped into the fray, organizing nurses and supplies to travel to the war zone at her own expense. At the same time, Sidney Herbert, who was now secretary at war, tapped her for help. Now she had government support, and suddenly to her mother, sister, and everyone else, she was Britain's heroine!

A desperately seasick Florence arrived in Scutari, Turkey, on November 4, 1854. She discovered a filthy hospital, ripe with open sewers, rats, and disease. The little food that was available included stale biscuits and boiled animal carcasses with only a tiny bit of meat still attached. On top of the horrid conditions, no orders for her or her nurses had been dispatched!

Florence carried on, writing detailed notes of the diseases, wounds, and problems with contaminated water. She set up shop the best she could, some days on her feet for more than 20 hours.

"I hope in a few days we shall establish a little cleanliness," she wrote. "But we have not a basin nor a towel nor a bit of soap nor a broom—I have ordered 300 scrubbing brushes . . . But one half of the Barrack is so sadly out of repair that it is impossible

AMERICA'S FIRST TRAINED NURSES

The nursing profession developed somewhat slower in America than in Europe. The first two officially trained American nurses were Harriet Newton Phillips and Linda Richards.

Harriet finished her nurse's training at the Woman's Hospital of Philadelphia sometime before 1870 after having worked as a volunteer during the Civil War. She did missionary work among the Sioux and Ojibwa tribes, as well as Presbyterian missionary work in San Francisco.

When Linda graduated from one of the first American nursing schools at the New England Hospital for Women and Children in 1873, there were no textbooks or final exams. The student nurses were not even allowed to learn the names of the drugs they gave their patients. A few years after graduation, Linda traveled to England, where she met Florence Nightingale and studied her system of nursing.

to use a drop of water on the stone floors, which are all laid upon rotten wood, and would give our men fever in no time . . . I am getting a screen now for the Amputations, for when one poor fellow who is to be amputated tomorrow, sees his comrade today die under the knife it makes impressions—and diminishes his chances."

Rev. Sydney Osborne described Florence during her time at Barracks Hospital, remarking, "It is a face not easily forgotten, pleasing in its smile . . . a quiet look of firm determination to every feature. . . . I can conceive her to be a strict disciplinarian; she throws herself into a work at its head. As such she knows well how much success must depend upon literal obedience to her every order."

Florence wrote frequent letters to the British government pleading for a sanitary commission to improve the hospital's conditions. When the commission finally arrived in 1855, they flushed the sewers, improved the drinking water, and carted away garbage, including a horse carcass discovered floating in the fresh water supply.

The death rate at the Barracks Hospital was 60 percent when Florence arrived. After the sanitary commission did its work, it was reduced to less than 1 percent. She eased the chaos with strict organization and sanitation work at the hospital.

Florence traveled across the Black Sea to observe the hospitals in Crimea. There she was nicknamed the Lady with the Lamp because she walked with her lantern during late-night rounds checking on wounded and sick soldiers. She fearlessly nursed those with disease and was stricken herself on May 12, 1855. Feverish and weak, she scribbled notes on hospital reform and the bungled war. Her nurses forced her to rest, and by August she was back at work. The war ended when Russia retreated from Crimea at the hands of France, Great Britain, and Turkey in 1856.

Florence's troubles during the Crimean War motivated the rest of her life. She established nursing methods, setting the standard for many years. In her book, *Notes on Nursing: What It Is, and What It Is Not*, she defined what was best for the patient.

After the war Florence had one year of good health. The Crimean fever (known as brucellosis, an infection caught from drinking the unpasteurized milk of infected animals) returned, and she was effectively bedridden for the rest of her life.

Modern-day antibiotics would have cured her, but they were not invented until 1928.

From her bedroom Florence calculated deaths and diseases, noting details about the illnesses, what cured them, what did not, and what could have been done differently. She invented a graphic to tell the story of the Crimean War called the Polar Area Diagram. Each month during the war, she recorded the numbers of soldiers who died from preventable causes compared with those who died from accidents and other events, all in various-colored wedges.

The blue wedges, which showed death from disease, shrunk dramatically after the 1855 sanitary commission had cleaned the sewage lines. Sanitation was the key. An obvious conclusion

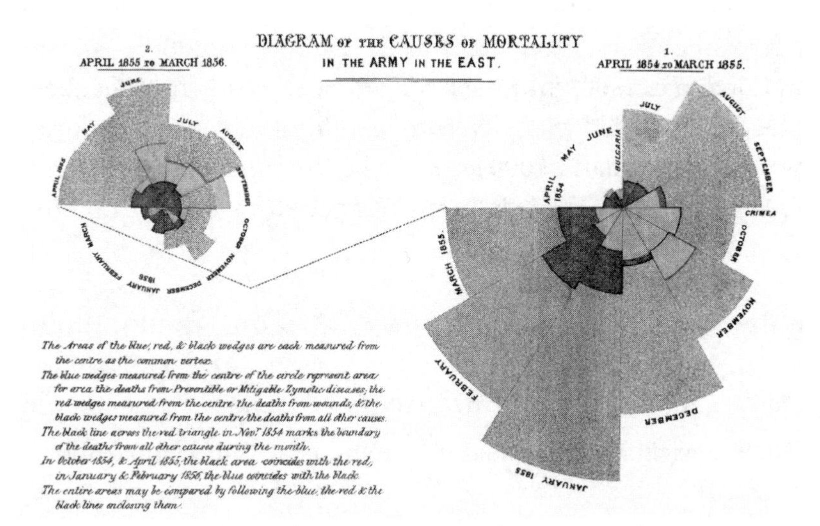

Florence Nightingale created the Polar Area Diagram to illustrate to government officials the large number of soldiers dying from preventable causes versus battlefield injuries. The "blue" wedges representing death from disease are the darkest ones shown above. The smaller diagram shows the shrinkage of disease deaths after she addressed simple hygiene measures. *Wikimedia Commons*

in our time, but in Florence's it was a relatively new thought. Using powerful graphics she made sense of the data, "to affect thro' the Eyes what we fail to convey to the public through their word-proof ears."

Florence was a noble nurse; however, her impact on nursing was greatest in the area of statistics and hospital reform. From her studies she changed the way hospitals were designed and operated, and by 1900 army deaths were fewer than civilian deaths. She believed that "statistics . . . is the most important science in the whole world, for upon it depends the practical application of every other [science] and of every art. To understand God's thoughts we must study statistics, for these are the measure of His purpose."

Though her illness continued, Florence's mind remained sharp. She opened the Nightingale Training School for nurses in London in 1860, running it for 27 years, mostly from her bed. She corresponded with government officials on hospital reform, writing more than 13,000 letters in her lifetime. Florence Nightingale died at her home in London at age 90, on August 13, 1910.

LEARN MORE

Florence Nightingale by Demi (Henry Holt, 2014)

Florence Nightingale by Shannon Zemlicka (Carolrhoda Books, 2003)

Florence Nightingale: The Courageous Life of the Legendary Nurse by Catherine Reef (Houghton Mifflin Harcourt, 2016)

Heart and Soul: The Story of Florence Nightingale by Gena K. Gorrell (Tundra Books, 2000)

Elizabeth Blackwell

Medical Pioneer

I do not wish to give [women] a first place, still less a second one—but the most complete freedom, to take their true place whatever it may be.

Nine-year-old Elizabeth smelled smoke. Fear gripped the girl as she looked outside from the window. It was October 29, 1830, and rioters protesting the treatment of the poor were torching the town. Two years earlier Samuel Blackwell's sugar refinery had burned down. He wasn't going to let that happen again, so he raced to protect this new refinery and other town buildings from the rioters.

Hours passed. Where was her father? Would he return unharmed? If only she were a boy, she thought, she would be free to search for him, help save the mill, and bring him home. Her father had fought hard for the passage of England's Reform Bill, which was proposed to allow representation of the middle

Elizabeth Blackwell.
Library of Congress

class in Parliament and take away the power of the rich landowners. Samuel was sympathetic with the protesters' cause, but he couldn't stop the riot. He stayed awake for days to protect his business.

Elizabeth Blackwell was born on February 3, 1821, in the town of Bristol, England. She was the third of nine children born to sugar refiner Samuel and his wife, Hannah. Samuel believed his daughters had just as much right to education as his sons did, an exceptional stance for fathers to take at the time. Avid reader Elizabeth had inherited her father's independence.

England's 1832 depression hit hard, and the family moved to America, settling in New York City. As abolitionists in England, the Blackwells had fought against slavery, and in the United States they joined the cause again.

One evening William Lloyd Garrison, a friend of Elizabeth's father, was at their home speaking against slavery. Elizabeth glanced around the room and noticed only she and Papa were engaged in the discussion. She couldn't understand how conversation drifted to babies, dresses, and dinners when human freedom was at stake! At 15 she began to attend antislavery meetings.

Samuel's New York sugar refinery failed and the family moved again, to Cincinnati, Ohio. Soon after the move, tragedy struck when Samuel Blackwell died from a weakened heart after getting his feet wet and cold on their journey. Elizabeth became the new leader of the family, and together they established a small school, barely making enough to support themselves.

When Elizabeth received an offer to teach in Henderson, Kentucky, earning $400 a year, she had to go. The small town and school were in pitiable shape, and although she had opposed slavery for many years, this was her first real exposure to it, living in a slaveholding state. She was horrified by the treatment of one slave girl who was asked to block the heat of the roaring fire so Elizabeth could stay cooler. She hated the injustice of slavery and returned to Cincinnati to devise a new plan.

Elizabeth had always avoided sickness and couldn't understand weakness of any kind. Yet she nursed her family often, and when her friend Mary was dying of cancer, she nursed her, too. Mary drew Elizabeth close and said, "You are fond of study, have health and leisure; why not study medicine? If I could have been treated by a lady doctor, my worst sufferings would have been spared me."

Elizabeth was shocked. How could she become a doctor? She thought about the idea, accepting and rejecting it several times over. Writing in her autobiography, she said, "I felt that I was severing the usual ties of life, and preparing to act against my strongest inclinations. But a force stronger than myself then and afterwards seemed to lead me on; a purpose was before me which I must inevitably seek to accomplish."

Her supportive family suggested she find a doctor with whom to study medicine. Most of the physicians she wrote to told her the idea was a good one but impossible to accomplish. Dr. John Dickson in North Carolina finally wrote back and offered her a teaching position and agreed to tutor her in the evenings. She moved to North Carolina and studied first with Dr. John Dickson in Ashville and then with his brother, Dr. Sam Dickson. In those two years, the more she learned, the more determined she was to achieve her goal of becoming a doctor.

Next Elizabeth wrote to a Dr. Warrington in Philadelphia, asking for more advice on the best way to become a physician. She waited months for a reply. He didn't think she would succeed but invited her to Philadelphia, the center of American medical studies, to discuss her mission. With each new doctor she met, she stated that she wanted to study medicine to aid the sick and injured. One physician, Dr. Parkhurst, offered to admit her to his classes, but only if she dressed like a man!

To enter into medicine in disguise was a repellant thought to Elizabeth. No, she would become a doctor honestly or not at all. She applied to the medical schools in Philadelphia and New York, plus 12 additional medical colleges. Each week passed with no word from the schools. The painful wait lasted for more than 16 weeks, until on October 20, 1847, a letter arrived.

> To Elizabeth Blackwell, Philadelphia, I am instructed by the faculty of the medical department of Geneva [New York] University to acknowledge receipt of yours of 3rd inst. A quorum of the faculty assembled last evening for the first time during the session, and it was thought important to submit your proposal to the class, who have had a meeting this day, and acted entirely on their own behalf, without any interference on the part of the faculty. . . . Wishing you success in your undertaking, which some may deem bold in the present state of society, I subscribe myself, Yours respectfully, Charles A. Lee, Dean of the Faculty.

Elizabeth had been accepted, but, as she found out later, the male students who approved her admission had thought the whole idea was a joke! They did not think she would enroll. She moved to Geneva, New York, to begin classes. On the first day, classmates, professors, and townspeople stared and whispered behind her back. Who was this strange woman in the midst of men studying to become physicians?

Elizabeth proved all doubters wrong, and on January 23, 1849, she walked with her brother Henry toward the Geneva College Presbyterian Church for the graduation ceremony. The streets were quiet, and she wondered where the town's women had gone. They had treated her as a curiosity and perhaps didn't approve, but she had hoped they would support her on this magnificent day.

A surprise waited for Elizabeth in the church. Her classmates were there, of course, but so were the women from the town, dressed in their finest clothes to watch the first woman doctor graduate from a traditional medical school in the United States!

After graduation Elizabeth did not feel ready to practice medicine on her own; she needed real experience. She traveled to Paris to study surgery, but even with important letters of introduction, every hospital she applied to said no. Once again it was suggested she disguise herself as a man to be accepted. Again she replied that she would study as a woman or not at all!

Her only hope to gain on-the-job experience was to begin at the bottom at La Maternité, a large hospital for pregnant women. No one recognized her degree as a doctor, and they placed her with the young French girls training to be midwives. Elizabeth boarded with these girls in a large dormitory, and although the conditions were poor, she was able to witness many deliveries.

Near the end of her six-month stay, on November 4, 1849, Elizabeth faced a new obstacle. As she was cleaning out the infected eye of a baby, some of the pus squirted into Elizabeth's left eye. Monsieur Blot, an intern with whom she'd become close, bandaged both eyes and sent her to bed immediately.

The strong infection caused her eyes to swell, and her vision was blurry at best. "For three weeks I lay in bed with both eyes closed, then the right eye began to open gradually." She was as optimistic as ever. Nothing had stopped her yet, but how could she operate with only one eye?

The diseased left eye needed to be removed. A famous oculist, Louis-Auguste Desmarres, replaced it with a glass eye, and as Elizabeth healed, new dreams came into focus. Surgery would be impossible, but she was still a doctor; she could still treat her patients.

While she was in England, Elizabeth met Florence Nightingale, another medical pioneer. They both believed in hospital reform, and Florence taught Elizabeth about the importance of sanitation, a new practice at the time.

THE ELIZABETH BLACKWELL AWARD

Each year the American Medical Women's Association gives the Elizabeth Blackwell Medal to an outstanding woman in medicine. The recipient must have made pathways for other women in medicine, have overcome adversity, have demonstrated originality and creativity in a medical field, and be recognized as a leader in women's health. The award was first given in 1949 to Mary Riggs Noble, MD, a medical missionary in India, and to date there have been 66 recipients.

Before Elizabeth left in 1851, Florence tried to persuade her to stay in Europe, but Elizabeth sensed that if she were to be men's equal, she must return to America. She must also return for her sister Emily, who had begun her medical education at the Cleveland Medical College.

Elizabeth set up practice in New York and waited for patients. The same prejudices that she had faced in medical school still existed now: no one wanted to see a woman doctor. She was called a "streetwalker" and a "woman of loose morals" all because she had entered the man's world of medicine. She hoped that by giving a series of lectures to young girls and their mothers, she would gain patients. Elizabeth stood in the front of the church near her practice and spoke on cleanliness and physical education for girls. She stated that "food, air, sleep, exert a chemical action upon the system" and were the key for a healthy life. The lectures were a success!

In 1854 she set up a dispensary to offer free care for the poor. People still gossiped. "These malicious stories are painful to me. . . . Ah, I am glad I, and not another, have to bear this pioneer work. I understand now why this life has never been lived before. I should like a little fun now and then. Life is altogether too sober."

A lonely Elizabeth lacked a good female friend tied to the medical world. Then one day a German midwife, Marie Zakrzewska, knocked on the dispensary door seeking advice. Elizabeth welcomed her. She taught Marie English and helped her gain admission to Cleveland Medical College.

Still feeling like something was missing from her life, 33-year-old Elizabeth adopted a seven-year-old Irish orphan, Kitty Barry. Elizabeth wrote, "Who will ever guess the restorative support which that poor little orphan has been to me? It was a dark time, and she did me good—her genial, loyal, Irish temperament suited me."

Elizabeth's sister Emily and friend Marie were now doctors. They joined Elizabeth in 1856 to open the New York Infirmary for Indigent Women and Children. Now in their own hospital, they could train as many female doctors as they wanted.

The American Civil War loomed. Elizabeth helped in forming the US Sanitary Commission to train nurses, set up and maintain shelters, and feed the soldiers. After the war she opened the Woman's Medical College of the New York Infirmary, setting high standards for admission and curriculum. Elizabeth took up the position of chair of hygiene and oversaw the work of the "sanitary visitor" sent to the homes of the poor. She believed the first lesson necessary for healthy children was to keep the household clean.

In 1869 Elizabeth felt that her work in America was finished. England was far behind in its medical education for women, so

Elizabeth Blackwell and her daughter, Kitty Barry Blackwell, in their study, 1905. *Harvard University, Schlesinger Library, Radcliffe Institute*

she worked with Sophia Jex-Blake and Elizabeth Garrett Anderson to open the London School of Medicine for Women in 1874. When Elizabeth became ill with biliary colic, a painful stomach virus, she decided to leave London for good.

She and Kitty moved to Hastings, England, in 1879, to Rock House. There Elizabeth looked out over the English Channel and read and wrote about reform and ways to make sure women succeeded as often as men. She died at the age of 89 on May 31, 1910.

A plaque hangs on a wall at Rock House with an excerpt from a Robert Browning poem. One change was made to the text—the change from "his" to "her" in the first line.

One who never turned her back but marched
breast forward
Never doubted clouds would break,
Never dreamed, though right were worsted, wrong
would triumph
Held we fall to rise, are baffled to fight better
Sleep to wake.
—Adapted from Asolando, Robert Browning, 1889

LEARN MORE

Elizabeth Blackwell: First Woman Physician by Tristan Boyer Binns (Franklin Watts, 2005)

Three 19th-Century Women Doctors: Elizabeth Blackwell, Mary Walker, and Sarah Loguen Fraser by Mary K. LeClair, Justin D. White, and Susan Keeter (Hofmann, 2007)

Women in Science: 50 Fearless Pioneers Who Changed the World by Rachel Ignotofsky (Ten Speed, 2016)

Clara Barton

Bold Angel

I may be compelled to face danger, but never fear it, and while our soldiers can stand and fight, I can stand and feed and nurse them.

On August 30, 1862, Clara Barton dressed in a plain dark skirt and blouse and climbed into one of the boxcars filled to the brim with food, blankets, and bandages she had collected. A battle was being fought near Manassas, Virginia, and, Clara said, her place during the Civil War was "anywhere between the bullet and the hospital."

The train trip lasted two hours, and when she finally arrived at her destination, a panicked Clara was unprepared for what she saw. She wrote, "At 10 o'clock Sunday our train drew up at Fairfax station. The ground for acres was a thinly wooded slope . . . and among the trees on the leaves and grass were laid the wounded who were pouring in by scores of wagon loads

Clara Barton, 1865.
Wikimedia Commons

as picked up on the field under flag of truce. All day they came and the whole hill side was covered."

Forty-year-old Clara did her best with few supplies. She recalled in her writings "how we put socks and slippers on their cold damp feet . . . wrapped blankets and quilts about them. And when we had no longer there to go, how we covered them in the hay and left them to their rest."

The only food available was what Clara had brought with her. She mixed up countless kettles of her own concoction. "Army crackers put into knapsacks and haversacks and beaten to crumbs between stones, and stirred into a mixture of wine or whiskey and water and sweetened with coarse brown sugar. Not very inviting you will think but I assure you always acceptable."

Clara Barton was born in 1821, in North Oxford, Massachusetts, the same year as another famous medical woman: Elizabeth Blackwell. Clara was as mighty and determined as Elizabeth and Florence Nightingale, who was born one year earlier.

The baby of the family by 11 years, Clara was raised by her brothers and sisters as much as her parents. They each took turns helping her with a special skill. One taught her to read, another taught her how to ride a horse, and her father told her countless war stories, sparing no details. Her mother was an abolitionist, and Clara learned that all people should have the same rights, including women!

At an early age, she stayed close to those who needed her, even the farm animals. When her brother David fell off the roof and broke both legs, Clara nursed him. Finally after two years, he walked again. Clara was at her best when she was needed.

As a young girl, she was shy and insecure, and her parents were worried she would never make it out in the world. They suggested that she might pursue teaching to gain confidence, but the thought of standing in front of a room full of students panicked her. Would they jeer? Would she run away in shame?

Teaching was considered one of the few "acceptable" careers for a woman in the early 1800s, and Clara passed her teaching certificate test when she was 17. Five-foot-tall Clara secured a position instructing a raucous class at a nearby school. Inside she was a bundle of nerves, but with her calm demeanor her new students listened to her and respect for her grew.

Clara demanded the same pay as male teachers, and at most places she received it. She founded a public school in Bordentown, New Jersey, and 600 students enrolled. The following term, the town decided that the school should be run by a man. The new principal was to be paid twice as much as Clara. She resigned immediately.

She moved to Washington, DC, where she met Charles Mason, head of the US Patent Office. He offered her a clerking job paying $1,400 per year, a very generous salary for a woman at the time. She cherished her new job and ignored the men who blew cigar smoke in her face.

When Charles Mason was replaced as the head of the office, Clara lost her job. But she had reinvented herself before and she set out to find a new reason to get up in the morning. Again and again she hit walls: men were not interested in hiring women.

There was nowhere else to go but home to North Oxford. Her savings dwindled, and sacrifices for her family wore her down, pushing her into a depression. Finally emerging, she wrote, "I must not rust much longer . . . but push out and do something somewhere, or anything, anywhere." She knew she didn't want to teach and wished to return to the lively environment of the US Patent Office.

In a letter to her nephew Bernard Vassall, Clara wrote, "I am naturally businesslike and habit has made me just as much so as a man. I should be 'perfectly happy' today if someone would tell me that my desk and salary were waiting for me—that once more I had something to do that *was* something."

When the US Patent Office recalled her at a reduced salary, she jumped at the chance. In 1860 the United States elected Abraham Lincoln as president just as the country teetered on the edge of war over states' rights and the issue of slavery. Many people, including Clara, believed there must be some way to keep the Union together.

The nation's political climate was changing, and Clara feared for her job. Those who had appointed her were no longer in power. She decided she must take action. She targeted one of Massachusetts's two senators, Henry Wilson, as an ally. One day she tied her bonnet and walked directly to the senate chambers and introduced herself. Certainly a bold move for a woman in 1861!

Fortunately Henry Wilson was interested in her complaint of the overcrowded conditions at the Patent Office. He favored seeing women in the office and believed they had something to offer. Were the tides turning for women's rights?

In Baltimore, Maryland, one week after the first shots of the Civil War were fired, an angry mob loyal to the South attacked the Sixth Massachusetts Regiment. Clara and her sister were determined to aid the wounded. But as the injured troops arrived from Baltimore, it was clear that the city of Washington was completely unprepared for war. Clara needed food, a hospital, and clean towels. She hired servants to carry wicker baskets full of donated supplies and set up shop in the senate chamber and her sister Sally's house.

Shortly after the Civil War began, 75,000 Union troops marched into Washington, changing the once small, quiet city into a lively place. The soldiers pitched white tents and marched in the streets. Clara had grown up listening to war stories on her father's lap. Now the war was in her own backyard, and it thrilled her. She called the roll of the drum "music I sleep by."

Clara wrote to her friends and family asking for any supplies they could spare. She placed advertisements in newspapers and became an expert in how to pack a box to ensure that clothes and food would be kept separate. Using her impressive organizational skills, she gathered supplies from towns and cities all over the region, and now her warehouses overflowed with soap, lemons, cloth, and honey. But her supplies were needed on the battlefield, not stuck in a warehouse. Would she be allowed near the fighting?

Barriers had never stopped her before, and after several refusals Colonel Daniel Rucker finally issued travel passes. Clara, a few attendants, and six wagons full of supplies traveled to Fredericksburg, Virginia, and into the turmoil of the Civil War.

Every battle she came upon told the same story: no supplies, no treatment in the field. Soldiers were dying unnecessarily of infection and lack of food or water. Clara didn't have any official nurse's training; she did what she could, jumping in wherever there was a need. At Antietam she provided basic care just behind the cannon, minutes after the fighting. It was here that she received her nickname, "Angel of the Battlefield."

Once when she held a cup for a wounded soldier to drink from, she felt a rustle in her sleeve and suddenly the soldier fell back dead. An enemy's bullet had passed through Clara's sleeve and into the soldier's back. One of many close calls!

Clara had found her purpose in the Civil War, along with her grit and need for excitement. A few years after the war ended, she ached to be needed again.

She traveled to Europe and met Dr. Louis Appia, learning of an organization called the International Committee of the Red Cross. The Red Cross was backed by the Geneva Treaty of 1864, which protected soldiers and their families during wars. She made a promise to him that one day she would add the United States to the International Red Cross roster.

Clara stayed in Europe until 1873, working for the International Red Cross. When she returned to the United States, her depression and anxiety problems returned. No matter how hard she worked, she felt she couldn't do enough. What did people think of her? Did she measure up? She couldn't sleep or eat, and suffered a nervous breakdown.

As she regained strength, she recalled the work of the International Red Cross. In 1877 Clara wrote to Dr. Appia to discuss setting up the American Red Cross Society. Dr. Appia wrote back within the month to tell her that the International Red Cross would welcome her assistance. The International Committee appointed her as their representative to Washington.

To further her cause, she wrote a booklet, *The Red Cross of the Geneva Convention: What It Is*, educating Americans on its purpose and describing how the Red Cross could help in peacetime as well as during war.

She met with officials in the US State Department, who didn't see a need for an American Red Cross. Why, they asked, would

THE RED CROSS

Swiss banker Jean Henri Dunant founded the International Red Cross in 1863. He had witnessed the aftermath of battle and wanted to help by creating a relief organization. In 1864 the Geneva Convention set out guidelines for prisoner of war treatment, as well as for protecting the sick and wounded.

It didn't matter what nationality the injured claimed, everyone had the right to care. Twelve European countries initially ratified these guidelines. The aid workers wore armbands of white with a red cross in the middle (a reversal of the Swiss flag), meaning they could not be fired on in battle.

Today the American Red Cross provides disaster relief by responding to 70,000 disasters in the United States every year, including hurricanes, floods, and earthquakes. The Red Cross facilitates blood donation for nearly four million people, generating almost half of America's blood supply. They teach CPR and basic first aid and assist the military with family resources and training for wounded soldiers.

America want to follow the Geneva Convention rules written by other countries? But Clara didn't quit and vowed to found the organization even without the government's approval.

Clara was elated when newly elected president James Garfield supported her effort. When he was assassinated in 1881, she feared she would have to begin again with President Chester Arthur. But he supported her, too, and signed the treaty on March 1, 1882. Her hard work was rewarded! She was named the president of the American Red Cross Society and served as its leader for the next 23 years.

At age 83, in 1904, Clara Barton resigned her presidency over rumors that she was living off Red Cross money. Nothing could have been further from the truth, and in fact she often spent her own money on Red Cross business. She was cleared of the accusations, and though she was deeply hurt, she still supported the organization.

Clara died on April 12, 1912, at her home in Glen Echo, Maryland.

LEARN MORE

Clara Barton: Angel of the Battlefield by Editors of TIME for Kids (Time for Kids Biographies, 2008)

Clara Barton: Courage Under Fire by Janet Benge and Geoff Benge (YWAM, 2002)

Clara Barton: Founder of the American Red Cross by Barbara Somervill (Compass Point Books, 2007)

Marie Zakrzewska

Woman's Spirited Ally

I prefer to be remembered only as a woman who was willing to work for the elevation of Woman.

Marie clutched her mother's skirts as she followed her through the wards. Her mother was a midwife, and because Marie had a serious eye infection leaving her sight impaired, she was allowed to stay with her mother at work. The "little blind doctor," as she was called, was pulled into a new and fascinating world.

As her eyes improved, Marie focused in on what she saw. "I learned all of life that it was possible for a human being to learn," she later wrote. "I saw . . . meanness in palaces, virtue among prostitutes and vice among so-called respectable women. I learned to . . . see goodness where the world found nothing but faults, and also to see faults where the world could see nothing but virtues."

Marie Zakrzewska, 1860.
Sophia Smith Collection, Smith College, Harvard University, National Library of Medicine

Marie Elizabeth was born on September 6, 1829, to Ludwig Martin Zakrzewska and Caroline Fredericke Wilhelmina Urban in Berlin, Germany. She was the eldest of five sisters and one brother. Her father's family has been traced back to AD 911 as one of Polish nobility. The family's fortune was lost to the Russians in territorial battles between Russia, Prussia, and Austria in 1793.

Following in her mother's path, Marie first applied to the Charité School of Midwifery in 1847 at age 18. They said she was too young and inexperienced and rejected her. She applied again one year later. Another rejection. In 1849 she was turned away for the third time. But she did not give up!

Marie knew the value of an ally and turned to Joseph Hermann Schmidt, associate professor of obstetrics at the school. He took her request all the way to King Frederick IV of Prussia. Whether it was thanks to the king or to Joseph's recent promotion to Charité's midwifery institution director, Marie finally began midwifery school in the fall of 1849.

Before she graduated, Joseph sought to promote Marie to head midwife, but he was forced to wait until she finished her studies. She was not well liked by the other professors; they believed she had a snippy nature and angered too easily. But she was not behaving any differently from the men. Her "fault" was that she was a woman.

She was finally appointed head midwife. Sadly just as she was about to start, her mentor and friend Dr. Joseph Schmidt died and so did not get to see her assume the position he knew she deserved. As head midwife Marie's duties included management of the maternity ward and instructing the midwifery and medical students. A woman teaching the medical students was considered improper, and to smooth the other professors' egos, she split her responsibilities with Catherine Stahl, the assistant to the head midwife.

Fits of jealousy from Catherine over their proposed duties led to Marie's resignation. She said, "I soon ceased to be the humble woman and spoke boldly what I thought, in defiance. . . . The end was, that I declared my readiness to leave the hospital."

At this time in Germany, a woman could attain no higher medical position than midwife. America was the only place Marie could become a doctor. Joseph Schmidt had once told her that in America science has no sex. She sailed with her younger sister Anna in April 1853 at the age of 23, with scarcely $100 and a "heart rich in faith and hope."

When the pair arrived in New York City, Marie wrote to Dr. Reisig, a doctor with whom her mother had worked. She had hoped he would invite her to run a midwifery business for him. Instead he offered her a job as a nurse. Marie walked away insulted, as she felt she was much more highly trained than a nurse. She formed her own midwifery practice in New York, but few patients knocked on the door. She needed money, more of it than her sister could earn sewing piecework 11 hours a day.

When Marie discovered the high price that fine worsted goods would command, she knew she had her business. She used what little money they had left and bought a small amount of fine Berlin wool with which to make tassels. "I then went to the office of a German newspaper, where I paid twenty-five cents for advertising for girls who understood all kinds of knitting. . . . In the evening when my sister came home, I was, therefore, safely launched into a manufacturing business." Eventually Marie employed 30 women making wool tassels to sell to clothing companies.

Marie had become a successful small-business operator, yet this was only a detour in her all-consuming desire to become a doctor. She had heard of Dr. Elizabeth Blackwell gaining admission to Geneva Medical College on a hoax and using it to her advantage. So she decided to pay a call on Elizabeth at her home in New York City.

Elizabeth answered her door and, soon after, Marie said, "From this call . . . I date my new life in America." After the meeting Elizabeth wrote her sister, Emily, saying, "Marie Zakrzewska, a German about twenty-six. . . . There is true stuff in her, and I shall do my best to bring it out."

Elizabeth Blackwell tutored Marie in English and helped her gain admission to the Cleveland Medical College, where Elizabeth's sister, Emily, had recently earned her degree. Marie began her studies during the winter term of 1854. She was the third woman in America to become a degreed physician.

But just as Elizabeth had learned, even a medical degree did not guarantee a job. After searching the city of New York for a room in which to practice, Marie found the cost too high, and what's more, most landlords would not let her place a sign in the front door announcing her practice. She wrote, "I finally gave up looking for a room, and accepted Dr. Elizabeth Blackwell's offer; to occupy her back parlor (the front one serving as her own office); of which I took possession on the 17th of April."

After medical school Marie became known as Dr. Zak, for she tired of teaching Americans how to pronounce her name. She joined the Blackwell sisters in their venture as a resident physician in the New York Infirmary for Indigent Women and Children. It was a good first step.

After two years, in 1859, Marie received an offer from the New England Female Medical College to serve as the chair of obstetrics. Marie left her home with the Blackwells' good wishes to advance the cause of women in medicine.

In 1860 she published her book *A Practical Illustration of "Woman's Right to Labor"; or, A Letter from Marie E. Zakrzewska, M.D., Late of Berlin, Prussia*. In it she wrote of women's images of themselves as weak, sentimental, and dependent. She knew that for women to succeed, they needed to take action and change this view of themselves.

During her three years at the college, Marie worked to improve the school. Its founder, Dr. Samuel Gregory, did not believe in modern science. When Marie requested the purchase of microscopes and thermometers, he refused her, saying they didn't want any "new-fangled European notions" and that they needed a doctor who could cure patients without this new science. Marie lost her patience with Samuel. She had higher standards and set out to open her own hospital.

In July 1862 she founded New England Hospital for Women and Children in a little house on Pleasant Street. Soon the initial 10 beds turned into many more, and the tiny hospital burst out of this and another house. Marie acquired land in Roxbury, Massachusetts, to build a new hospital. The hospital was the first in America to provide medical care to women by women.

The Civil War brought a great shortage of nurses to aid the soldiers in battle. After the war Marie responded and opened the first American school for nurses within her hospital, where Linda Richards became America's first trained nurse.

Marie purchased a house with money from the hospital's board for her growing family. Two younger sisters stayed with her from time to time as their mother and then their father had died. Marie never married and instead formed her own untraditional family. While in Cleveland she had met and befriended Karl Heinzen, a radical German reformer who believed in women's rights. He and his wife were to live with Marie for many years, along with her lifelong companion, Julia A. Sprague. The house at 139 Cedar Street was a happy one, with many visitors and evenings filled with games of chess or whist, an English card game.

The years at the hospital were difficult, especially with a growing household to support. Marie worked long hours tending the poor, many of whom could not pay her. She wrote, "The excess of work was absolutely needed to dispel the prejudice against woman's ability to do night work. In January, 1864, I walked to the poor quarters in Roxbury five nights with the thermometer 8 and 10 degrees below zero. . . . It was my determination to prove that a woman has not only the same, but more physical endurance than man."

Marie pushed women to become scientific thinkers and not rely on traditional female qualities of comfort and nurture to care for the sick. She believed women must think as male physicians or they wouldn't succeed. She was an early member of the New England Women's Club, which promoted suffrage, education, and good health.

Marie practiced in Boston from 1859 to 1899 and earned the respect of many physicians and patients. One man, after bringing his ailing daughter to be treated by Marie, said, "When I

THE NEW ENGLAND WOMEN'S CLUB

The New England Women's Club was the first women's club in the United States. It was founded at the home of Dr. Harriot K. Hunt, who is considered the first American woman to practice medicine, although she never earned a degree. The first official meeting of the club was held on May 30, 1868, in Boston with the purpose of educating women and fueling their efforts for social causes. The weekly meetings consisted of speakers in history, literature, art, and current-interest topics such as women's suffrage and improving the health of homes and schools. Louisa May Alcott and suffragist Lucy Stone were early leaders. The club provided an outside meeting place for women when it was considered radical for women to even leave their homes or call their group a "club."

looked into that woman's face, I knew that my daughter was saved."

Through all of her hard work, Marie was still happy in the simplest of pleasures. She wrote, "The ocean is blue like the Mediterranean today; a cool breeze tempers the heat of the sun, while roses render the air fragrant, and wild flowers abound. Life is so beautiful when wants are moderate and the heart is open to the joys of nature."

Marie's efforts spurred many women to action as she educated two generations of female physicians. She died from a stroke in 1902 at the age of 72. The hospital she founded still exists in South Boston and is known today as the Dimock Community Health Center.

In her autobiography, *A Woman's Quest*, she wrote, "We stood no longer alone as the bearers of an idea—hundreds of young women had joined us. The path had been broken; and the profession had been obliged to yield, and to acknowledge the capacity of women as physicians."

LEARN MORE

Send Us a Lady Physician: Women Doctors in America, 1835–1920 by Ruth J. Abram (W. W. Norton, 1985)

Rebecca Lee Crumpler and Rebecca Cole

The First African American Women Physicians

My chief desire in presenting this book is to impress upon somebody's mind the possibilities of prevention.

—REBECCA LEE CRUMPLER

Many of the early women in medicine left written accounts of their lives, but for those who didn't, establishing the basic facts about them can be difficult. This is especially true when their experiences were discounted or uncorroborated or when only partial or inconsistent accounts remain. This is the case with the women thought to be the first two female African American physicians, Rebecca Lee Crumpler and Rebecca Cole. Few records of their lives remain, and there are no known photos of either of them. (The photo that is most often identified as Rebecca Crumpler is actually of Mary Eliza Mahoney, the first

African American nurse.) Because less is known about their life stories, these two groundbreakers are discussed together in this chapter.

It was difficult enough for a white woman to become a physician in the mid-1800s, but for African American women, the obstacles were even greater. Since women were not allowed the right to vote until 1920, they had no say in making laws. Only single women could own property, and once they married everything they owned became their husband's under the law. African American women, who weren't even considered citizens until the passage of the 14th Amendment in 1868, had fewer rights than white women.

The first medical school to accept black students, Howard University Medical School, opened in 1868. Until that time, most African American applicants, especially women, were denied admission to medical colleges and universities.

A medical education in the 1800s was quite different from one today. Often those interested in medicine simply took a course or two and declared themselves doctors without ever attending college. There were many different levels of medical education, with only some accredited by state boards. Women were held to the highest standards with the most difficult curriculum or they wouldn't be taken seriously. In other words, women, and especially black women physicians, had to check all the boxes and then some!

A "regular" medical school treated diseases through the use of drugs, surgery, or a combination and was accredited by a state board of examiners. Eclectic (treatment with plants and herbs) or homeopathic (treatment to mimic the symptoms the patient is already having) medical schools also existed, and these were called "irregular" medical schools. These schools didn't follow state standards and varied widely in their curricula.

HOWARD UNIVERSITY MEDICAL SCHOOL AND MEHARRY MEDICAL COLLEGE

The Howard University Medical School was founded in 1868 with the purpose of training African Americans for the medical profession. During its early years, though, it actually trained more white students than black, and they were mostly men. Howard University was often criticized for its gender-blind policy, meaning women could be admitted; however, the few who were admitted were white.

Meharry Medical College in Nashville, Tennessee, was founded a few years later in 1876. By 1920 it had graduated 39 black women physicians; the first of these were Annie Gregg and Georgia Esther Lee Patton, who graduated in 1893. But it was the Woman's Medical College of Pennsylvania's black female graduates who paved the way for many African American women in medicine. Their successes were thought to be greater because of both the high-quality education and the female faculty at the school. And many of the college's students came from influential, well-educated black families living in the North. By the end of the 19th century, the Woman's Medical College had graduated a dozen black women physicians.

The New England Female Medical College in Boston was founded in 1848, and its founder, Samuel Gregory, did not have formal medical training. It was considered an irregular medical

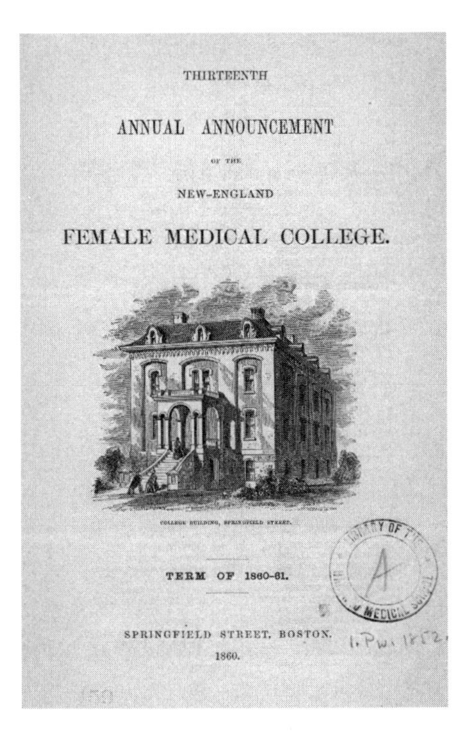

THIRTEENTH

ANNUAL ANNOUNCEMENT

OF THE

NEW-ENGLAND

FEMALE MEDICAL COLLEGE.

TERM OF 1860-61.

SPRINGFIELD STREET, BOSTON.

1860.

New England Female Medical College Annual Report, 1860. *Harvard University*

school. Originally a midwifery school for women, it was expanded to offer a full medical education. Samuel Gregory insisted on calling the degree doctress of medicine, chosen to appeal to women's supposed softer side. He proposed the problem of a male making an appointment to see a doctor and finding a woman attending him. A woman physician was such a new thought, he determined, that she must have her own title. Women physicians reacted negatively to being treated differently, and the "doctress" title did not catch on with other medical schools. Still, many influential women graduated from Samuel's unchartered medical school and forged their medical careers.

Rebecca Lee entered the New England Female Medical College in the 1859–1860 term as one of 22 students. The school's admission requirement was only that candidates "must satisfy the Faculty that they are of unexceptionable moral character, and that they possess a good preparatory education."

When Rebecca graduated on March 2, 1864, the *Daily Evening Traveller* reported the event, saying, "It is certainly very appropriate for the times. A wide field is open before [Lee], and many of her sisters, among the four millions of her people in our country, with their new future before them." Given the fact that she had to overcome discrimination for being a woman and African American, Rebecca's graduation in 1864 was an astonishing feat.

Most of the biographical information known about Rebecca comes from her 1883 book, *A Book of Medical Discourses: In Two Parts*. The dedication reads, "to Mothers, Nurses, and all who may desire to mitigate the afflictions of the human race, This Book is prayerfully offered." It is one of the first medical publications written by an African American and covers such topics as the care of a newborn, proper diet, and treatment of common diseases of the time, such as diphtheria and measles.

Rebecca Lee was born free in Delaware on February 8, 1831, to Absolum Davis and Matilda Weber. She was raised by an aunt in Pennsylvania. As a child she witnessed the loving care her aunt gave to others. Rebecca said in her book, "It may be well to state here that, having been reared by a kind aunt in Pennsylvania, whose usefulness with the sick was continually sought, I early conceived a liking for, and sought every opportunity to be in a position to relieve the sufferings of others."

Rebecca moved to Charleston, Massachusetts, when she was 21 and worked as a nurse for eight years. At this time nurses did not need degrees, and her training occurred on the job mostly through trial and error. The first formal nursing school, founded by Marie Zakrzewska, did not open until 1873 at the New England Medical Hospital for Indigent Women and Children in Boston.

The doctors Rebecca worked for wrote letters recommending her for admission to the New England Female Medical College in 1860. The American Civil War interrupted her studies, and when Rebecca returned in 1863, she was out of money. Fortunately she received a scholarship though the Wade Scholarship Fund, established by abolitionist Benjamin Wade. In 1864, armed with the degree doctress in medicine, she set up general practice in Boston.

Rebecca married escaped slave Arthur Crumpler, said to be a blacksmith who shod Union horses during the Civil War. When the Civil War ended in 1865, the couple moved to Richmond, Virginia, the former capital of the Confederate States of America. What Rebecca found there was a burned-out city full of needy people. Food was scarce, and many buildings and businesses had been destroyed as the Confederate troops retreated and the Union troops moved in. Rebecca offered urgent care to former slaves and worked for the Freedmen's Bureau. She wrote

THE FREEDMEN'S BUREAU

As the Civil War drew to a close, Abraham Lincoln knew he had to do something to help newly freed slaves. With lives no longer controlled by slave owners, the free Americans needed help finding work, medical care, and education. Reconstruction was the process to help reunite the Northern and Confederate states after the Civil War. Abraham Lincoln established the Freedmen's Bureau in 1865 as part of Reconstruction. More than 1,000 schools were built throughout the South. The bureau trained new teachers to educate the former slaves, assisting them in securing jobs and medical care.

that Richmond was the "proper field for real missionary work, and one that would present ample opportunities to become acquainted with the diseases of women and children."

Rebecca wrote of her time in Richmond, "During my stay there nearly every hour was improved in that sphere of labor. The last quarter of the year 1866, I was enabled . . . to have access each day to a very large number of the indigent, and others of different classes, in a population of over 30,000 colored."

Rebecca felt useful in Richmond but also endured extreme racism there. She had difficulty filling prescriptions, and male doctors claimed that the MD after her name stood for mule driver. But she was a respected physician in her community and was well known for her persistence in treating diseases suffered by women and children.

After several years in Richmond, Rebecca and Arthur moved back to Boston. Rebecca established her practice and residence at 20 Garden Street, where her patients again consisted of needy women and children. She worked "with renewed vigor, practicing outside, and receiving children in the house for treatment; regardless, in a measure, of remuneration." She believed wholeheartedly that prevention was the key to a long life, writing, "They seem to forget that there is a *cause* for every ailment, and that it may be in their power to remove it."

Good nutrition and cleanliness as vital to good health were new ideas in the mid-1800s, and Rebecca proposed guidelines in her book: "Washing is the name given to the old method. Cleansing is the proper name for the new. How to proceed: A soft, white, all wool blanket, about two yards square, should be always in readiness when a birth is expected. . . . As many babes have open eyes as soon born, it is best to dip a small piece of the soft linen or cotton in (fresh hog's lard or sweet oil), to clean the face, ears, nose—avoiding the eyes—neck, chest, under the arms and between the fingers." Today it seems hard to imagine that people needed to be told how to wash!

Rebecca practiced medicine until 1880, when she moved to Hyde Park, Massachusetts, with her husband. She was a true pioneer. She fought racism by conquering obstacles along the path to improving others' lives. She died on March 9, 1895, at the age of 64 in Fairview, Massachusetts.

Rebecca Cole was the second African American woman to earn her degree as a physician. She was rumored to have practiced before getting a medical license.

Rebecca was born in Philadelphia, Pennsylvania, the second of five children, on March 16, 1846. Her ancestry was a blend of European and African. Like many of the early medical women, she had the benefit of a strong education. She worked hard in school and was an excellent student who studied mathematics, Latin, and Greek at the Institute for Colored Youth. She once won a $10 prize for her hard work.

Rebecca gained admission to the Woman's Medical College of Pennsylvania and graduated in 1867 at the age of 21. Unlike Rebecca Lee Crumpler, Rebecca Cole graduated from a chartered medical school, studying a more rigorous course. She focused on the eyes and completed her thesis, titled *The Eye and Its Appendages.*

She moved to New York to join the Blackwell sisters, Elizabeth and Emily, both doctors at the New York Infirmary for Indigent Women and Children. Elizabeth Blackwell had formed the US Sanitary Commission, something she'd dreamed of doing for years. Rebecca was to become a "sanitary visitor" whose purpose was to check in with poor women of all races and assess their general health. This visitor might make suggestions in diet, cleaning, and care of the children in the household. While many doctors believed high death rates among the poor

Woman's Medical College of Pennsylvania, 1850. *Wikimedia Commons*

were because of ignorance, Rebecca claimed their crowded living conditions contributed to serious illness and eventual death.

Elizabeth said of the new doctor, "This post was filled by one of our assistant physicians, whose special duty it was to give simple, practical instruction to poor mothers on the management of infants and the preservation of the health of their families. An intelligent young coloured physician, Dr. Cole, who was one of our resident assistants, carried on this work with tact and care." The US Sanitary Commission was an experiment for the Blackwell sisters. Their Tenement House Service, begun in 1866, was one of the first medical social service programs in the United States.

Rebecca moved to Columbia, South Carolina, during Reconstruction, where there were many poor African American women and children. She knew she could improve their health. A few years later, she returned to Philadelphia and opened a

Women's Directory Center with Dr. Charlotte Abbey. This center provided legal and medical services for poor women and children.

In 1899 the Association for the Relief of Destitute Colored Women appointed Rebecca superintendent of a home. She was said to have possessed "all the qualities essential to such a position—ability, energy, experience, tact. . . . She has carried out her plans with the good sense and vigor which are a part of her character, while her cheerful optimism, her determination to see the best in every situation and in every individual, have created around her an atmosphere of sunshine that adds to the happiness and well-being of every member of the large family."

Rebecca Cole practiced medicine for 50 years and died on August 14, 1922, at the age of 76.

Although Rebecca Lee Crumpler and Rebecca Cole made great headway against discrimination, the odds continued to be against all African Americans. In the quarter century after the Civil War, 115 black women had become physicians. These physicians were a vital part of the communities in which they practiced. As black medical schools, such as Howard University and Meharry Medical College, struggled to find funds, most of their graduates continued to be men.

The number of black women physicians began to drop, and the 1920 census listed just 65 in practice. It took 50 years for the number to grow to 1,051 and by 1989 to 3,250. One of the biggest problems for African American women doctors came after they graduated. There were few hospitals that allowed any woman to train, and as Elizabeth Blackwell had learned 70 years earlier, a degree wasn't worth anything without good clinical training.

Trailblazers such as Rebecca Lee Crumpler and Rebecca Cole aided other black women in medicine. The third African American woman physician, Dr. Susan Smith McKinney

Steward, founded the Brooklyn Women's Homeopathic Hospital and Dispensary in 1881. And others, such as Sarah G. Jones and Lucy Hughes Brown, founded training schools and black hospitals in Richmond, Virginia, and Charleston, South Carolina, respectively, to help poor women and children.

LEARN MORE

African American Healers by Clinton Cox (John Wiley and Sons, 2000)

Mary Edwards Walker

Gutsy Surgeon in Pants

I am the original new woman. . . . Why, before Lucy Stone, Mrs. Bloomer, Elizabeth Cady Stanton and Susan B. Anthony were—before they were, I am. . . . I have made it possible for the bicycle girl to wear the abbreviated skirt, and I have prepared the way for the girl in knickerbockers.

Although she was working in the midst of Civil War, there were not enough sick or wounded Union soldiers in Gordon's Mills, Georgia, for Union Army volunteer and assistant surgeon Dr. Mary Walker to treat. Feeling idle, she asked for permission to deliver the babies and treat the illnesses of nearby Confederate civilians.

On April 10, 1864, Mary accidentally took the wrong road and, crossing enemy lines, was captured by the Confederates, who believed her to be a Union spy. She was held prisoner at

Dr. Mary Edwards Walker, Civil War surgeon, in her dress pants uniform. *Library of Congress*

Castle Thunder Prison, so named because it was said to have evoked the thunder of the gods. Mary's filthy bed in the Confederate prison was alive with bedbugs. She was allowed one meal a day, usually a slice of moldy bread and maggot-infested rice. She did her best to cope.

Mary was born on November 26, 1832, the fifth of six children, to Alvah and Vesta Walker. Her freethinking father believed education was important for both boys and girls. And since his five girls were kept busy with farm chores, he believed they shouldn't have to wear impractical clothing.

From the time when she worked on her family's farm, Mary knew what a hindrance women's clothing could be. Tight corsets made it difficult to breathe; long skirts collected dirt and dust; and hoops that stuck out made hard work out of walking. Alvah and Vesta broke all the rules by allowing their daughters to wear lightweight, loose cotton dresses. In fact they forbade their daughters to wear corsets and any garments that would constrict their blood.

Abolitionist Alvah Walker made a deep impression on his daughter. He filled her mind with ideas that she was as smart and strong as any man. Twenty-three-year-old Mary was the only woman to graduate from Syracuse Medical School in 1855. When she married another physician, Albert Miller, she refused to take his name, which was extremely rare at that time. The couple set up a medical practice in Rome, New York, and practiced together for four years. Patients were few, and many wondered who would go to a female doctor. Their marriage crumbled when Albert was unfaithful, and Mary pursued a life of her own.

Meanwhile, the future of the United States was in jeopardy. As the country grew, the Southern states thought any new territories should allow slavery, while the North thought the new territories should be slave free. Tension grew, and 11 Southern states seceded from the Union, forming the Confederate States of America. The American Civil War began when the first shots were fired on Fort Sumter on April 12, 1861.

Twenty-nine-year-old Mary traveled to Washington, DC, to request a commission in the army. The shortage of doctors to treat the wounded was severe, and Mary offered to help. She approached Dr. J. N. Green in the US Patent Office building, which had been turned into a makeshift hospital called Indiana Hospital. He was in dire need of help and welcomed Mary to his staff. She asked him to write a letter to Dr. Clement A. Finley, the surgeon general, so that he may give her a formal commission and a surgeon's pay. Most people in those days believed that it was improper for a woman to even appear in a hospital with strange men, let alone work as a surgeon.

Mary personally delivered the letter to Clement Finley's office. He read the letter and Mary's credentials and replied that he couldn't possibly appoint a woman as a surgeon. Mary also asked the advice of the assistant surgeon general, Robert C. Wood, who said that if his boss had been absent when she appeared, he might have appointed her assistant surgeon. But now that the decision had been made, he could not go against his boss's ruling. Mary returned to Indiana Hospital and volunteered without an appointment as an assistant surgeon. She still hoped her commission would come through, and when it didn't and she was still unpaid, she decided to leave the hospital and Dr. Green.

The Civil War was lasting much longer than anyone believed it would. Mary couldn't stay away even if she had to work for free. The Battle of Antietam was a gruesome battle with 22,717 wounded or killed, and Mary traveled to Warrenton, Virginia, to treat the wounded and the sick. As Florence Nightingale discovered during the Crimean War, many more soldiers were struck down from disease than from battle wounds. Typhoid was the deadliest of these diseases, and Mary asked for permission to transport the sickest of these soldiers to Washington, DC.

Major General Ambrose E. Burnside sent out an order commanding that "Dr. Mary E. Walker be authorized to accompany and assist in caring for, from Warrenton Virginia to Washington D. C., the sick and wounded soldiers now at the former post. The surgeon in Charge there will afford every facility to Dr. Walker for that purpose."

But first she must take care of the soldiers' immediate needs. Lacking many basic supplies, Mary searched for a washbasin and rags to place on the feverish soldiers' foreheads. She found the washbasin but wondered what she would use for towels. She wrote in her journal, "A brilliant idea had commenced to rush through my mind, the next one was to tear up a long night dress

I had with me into pieces about a foot square for towels. I called a well soldier, directing him to wash the faces and hands of the sick who were not able when the water was brought to them to wash themselves, and also to take clean water for every one of them: and after distributing my towels to them I rested while I observed the carrying out of my directions."

Tearing up one's own nightgown was a scandalous act for the time. It was believed that women of class and substance simply did not do what Mary had done! Mary didn't care what others thought of her; she only wished to be of service.

Throughout her war service, Mary fought to be recognized as a doctor and not a nurse. One newspaperman applauded her efforts, saying, "Her reputation is unsullied, and she carries herself amid the camp with a jaunty air of dignity well calculated to receive the sincere respect of the soldiers. She can amputate a limb with the skill of an old surgeon, and administer medicine equally as well."

For all of the praise and attention she received, Mary was still without a commission and without pay. Failure to achieve a formal appointment with the Union Army was unacceptable. She was as capable as any man.

Mary wrote to President Abraham Lincoln to request an appointment to serve at a Washington hospital, but again she was denied. The president did not want to interfere within the army's medical department; however, he did say that if they approved of her work, then he would agree, but only if she were to work in a ward with only female patients.

Congressman John Farnsworth had taken notice of her efforts and sent Mary to an interview of sorts to determine if she was qualified. The medical board at the Department of Cumberland (one of the principal Union armies) pronounced her capable of nursing but wondered whether she had actually studied medicine. Mary was outraged. She had been down this road before.

The scarcity of doctors at this point in the war caused alarm. Colonel Daniel McCook, who had seen Mary in action before, appointed her a contract surgeon with the 52nd Ohio Volunteer Infantry. Mary treated war wounds and performed amputations, but in almost every case she believed the amputation to be both unnecessary and "wickedly cruel." She earned $80 per month, much less than the $130 a man would have earned as an assistant surgeon. She was still without a formal commission, but at least she was being paid for her work in Gordon's Mills, Georgia.

After Mary tread deep into the woods across enemy lines, was captured, and accused of spying for the Union, she refused to admit to anything. But in an earlier letter she had written to the secretary of war, it appeared she had offered to spy: "I again offer my services to my country . . . for the relief of our sick soldiers and then use the style that I invented to give you information as their forces and plans and any important information."

DRESS REFORM

When the first women's rights convention occurred in 1848, dress reform was just beginning. Full skirts made walking difficult and climbing steps nearly impossible. The hoop skirt was a steel contraption worn underneath a woman's skirt to make it appear even fuller. It swung freely on the wearer and often knocked things or people over if she made a quick move. Dr. Mary Walker believed dresses were dishonest; they denied that women had legs!

continued on next page . . .

Excruciatingly tight corsets distorted the spine and compressed the lungs. A "weary soul in a weary frame," wrote the *Lily*, a woman's newspaper. Women such as Amelia Jenks Bloomer and Elizabeth Smith Miller experimented with a type of wide pant or Turkish pantaloons to be worn under a skirt about four inches below the knee. Society criticized this new way of dressing, but freethinking women wore them anyway, including Mary Walker.

During the American Civil War, Mary's dress was often discussed. She had designed a military outfit for her service, gold-striped pants as an officer would wear, the green sash of a surgeon, and a gold-corded hat. After the Civil War, in 1866, Mary was elected president of the National Dress Reform Association and was arrested several times for dressing as a man. She lectured throughout the country and told a reporter from the *Omaha Daily Bee* in 1875, "We have no trailing dress to draw along the sidewalk to be torn by nails, or stepped on by clumsy men; we do not have any garments to lift while crossing a street on a muddy day, and thus a woman need not expose her lower limbs to the prurient gaze of the corner loafer."

She fought for her release from prison by writing letters to the newspaper and after four months was freed in exchange for the release of a Confederate surgeon. She was delighted with the terms, for it was the first time a woman had been traded for an officer!

But her time in prison had taken its toll, especially with the health of her eyes, so Mary worked at a female prison in

Kentucky and at an orphan's asylum until the war ended on April 9, 1865.

Mary's greatest honor came when she was recommended for and granted a Congressional Medal of Honor by President Andrew Johnson. Dr. Mary E. Walker, a graduate of medicine, the president's commendation read, "has rendered valuable service to the Government, and her efforts have been earnest and untiring in a variety of ways."

Mary fought to receive a pension from the army, but the records showed that she worked as a nurse, not a surgeon. The government sent her $8.50 a month, much less than the $50 per month that soldier's widows received. Would she ever get her reward? Thirty-three years after the war ended, she finally received $20 a month from the government.

When Congress changed the requirements for the Medal of Honor in 1916, requiring service with actual combat, Mary's award was withdrawn. She was crushed and vowed to never return the medal, wearing it every day for the rest of her life. She died on February 21, 1919. President Jimmy Carter restored her medal in 1977.

LEARN MORE

Civil War Doctor: The Story of Mary Walker by Carla Johnson (Morgan Reynolds, 2007)

A Woman of Honor: Dr. Mary E. Walker and the Civil War by Mercedes Graf (Thomas Publications, 2001)

Mary Edwards Walker: Above and Beyond by Dale L. Walker (Tom Doherty Associates, 2005)

PART II
Medical Women Making Headway

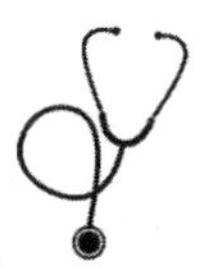

A measure of victory has been won, and honors have been bestowed in token thereof. But honors fade or are forgotten, and monuments crumble into dust. It is the battle itself that matters—and the battle must go on.

—ELIZABETH KENNY

The bold female medical pioneers of the 19th century paved the way for women of the 20th century to make even greater headway. The Civil War had proved an effective training ground, but there were still unforeseen battles.

In the early 1900s, wealthy families such as the Carnegies and Rockefellers began to use their fortunes for medical reform. The Carnegie Foundation hired educator Abraham Flexner (a man with no background in medicine) to judge the quality of medical schools. By this time most states had set more rigorous standards for their medical schools, and the more prestigious schools received more money, enabling them to buy better equipment and hire more desirable teachers.

Abraham visited 155 schools, targeting those that were deemed inferior because of inadequate academics and laboratory facilities. He also believed that most of the inferior schools accepted students who were unqualified to study medicine. In addition he came to the conclusion that medical colleges for women had no reason to stay open since women could easily attend medical colleges alongside men. However, many medical schools still rejected women. The 1910 *Flexner Report* criticized nearly every medical school except for Johns Hopkins, which was held up as the model. The report had such an ill effect that within 10 years only 85 of the 155 schools Abraham visited remained open. Two out of the three medical colleges for women did not survive, and by 1920 all but one (Woman's Medical College of Pennsylvania) had closed or merged with another college.

Still, despite the consequences of the *Flexner Report*, women continued to advance, slowly, in medical careers. Much of this was due to the rapid growth in hospitals. There had been fewer than 200 hospitals in the United States in 1873. Within four decades, in 1910, there were over 4,000. This increase drew medical women out of the home and into the workplace.

The women of this section (with the exception of Susan La Flesche Picotte, due to her premature death) lived during a time when they had achieved the right to vote. Even with the vote, the number of female medical students took a sharp dip in the early 1900s, from 1,280 in 1902 to 992 in 1926. And by 1929, 13,174 men had applied to medical schools, compared with only 481 women. In her book *"Doctors Wanted, No Women Need Apply": Sexual Barriers in the Medical Profession, 1835–1975*, Mary

Roth Walsh speculates that the fight for women's suffrage took so much focus that it partially deflated the focus of professional women, including those interested in medicine.

Other events shared by medical women in the early 20th century (again except for Susan La Flesche Picotte) were World Wars I and II, which opened up new opportunities for them. Nurses, physicians, and other medical professions were needed just as they had been during the Civil War. At the beginning of America's involvement in World War I, 403 women nurses were on active duty as part of the US Army Nurse Corps. Women physicians had limited roles as contract physicians, much like Mary Walker had during the Civil War. The same was true at the beginning of World War II. Some female physicians and nurses were frustrated with US policies and served instead for the foreign countries of Great Britain and France. But as World War II continued, the shortage of battle-ready physicians became too great, and Congress passed legislation allowing women to serve in the army and navy medical corps. The first woman commissioned into the US Army Medical Corps was Dr. Margaret D. Craighill. She was given the rank of major.

To entice men to study medicine during the war, the government offered them free tuition; however, women were forced to pay their own bills. But by the end of the war in 1945, over 14 percent of first-year medical students were women. As soon as the war was over and the need had lessened, medical schools began to reduce their quotas for women students, and many medical schools did not have even one female student listed on their roster.

Through these ups and downs in the first half of the 20th century, this group of women carried on. They educated themselves either through formal or informal education, as in Elizabeth Kenny's on-the-job training in the Australian bush country.

When they were ready, they set up practices in unfamiliar places. And when they ran into walls, they scaled them by fund-raising, performing medical research, or even discovering a new view by changing jobs.

These women championed themselves and their distinctness from men in medicine. Bertha Van Hoosen wrote in her 1947 autobiography, *Petticoat Surgeon*: "A century ago the strongest argument against women in medicine was that its study would tend to make a woman coarse and barren of all feminine charms. No reasoning could be more fallacious, for the study of medicine develops tenderness, sympathy, tolerance, and benevolence."

When Bertha Van Hoosen organized the American Medical Women's Association in 1915, women finally had support from their own kind, easing their paths a little. No longer were women content with just basic care of the sick or wounded. They discovered treatments and cures for common diseases and birth defects, such as polio, or heart defects. They traveled by horseback and stagecoach or by more modern methods of train, car, and airplane. They toiled tirelessly, often forgetting to eat, drink, or sleep. Their paths may have been uncertain or difficult, but fear didn't stop them.

Mary Breckinridge embraced the roughness of the Appalachian Mountains to help isolated families. Susan La Flesche Picotte was always available to help her people, not only medically but also in everyday life. Sister Elizabeth Kenny did what she thought would help paralyzed polio victims; many walked again through her often-controversial treatments. Helen Taussig worked with "blue babies" to correct their birth defects, while Virginia Apgar realized the immediate need for assessing the health of newborns.

Each woman's effort made her patients' lives, and ultimately ours, easier.

Bertha Van Hoosen

Unstoppable Petticoat Surgeon

Perhaps I was different. On the farm I had learned how to meet realities without suffering either mentally or physically. . . . I had freedom to succeed—freedom to fail. Life on the farm produces a kind of toughness.

Bertha hung on the fence watching her father sharpen his knife on the grindstone. "The belly of the hog was expertly slashed from tail to snout with a big knife," she later wrote in her autobiography, *Petticoat Surgeon*. "The purple liver, crimson heart and spongy lungs rolled, a trembling mass, into the big dishpan. . . . Then came the work of the sharp ax, and the huge empty carcass was converted into hams, shoulders, tenderloins, ribs, pigs' feet, hunks of fat for salt pork and pieces for sausage. . . . I reveled in seeing what was under the skin."

Bertha Van Hoosen was born to Joshua and Sarah Van Hoosen on March 26, 1863, in Stony Creek, Michigan. Her father lacked a formal education but still believed in a strong educational foundation for his daughters, Alice, born eight years earlier, and Bertha. They attended public schools and graduated from high school in Pontiac, Michigan. Bertha followed her sister to the University of Michigan's English department.

After her graduation in 1884, Bertha's mother pleaded with her to become a teacher or move home to the farm. But Bertha had sampled a few medical courses at the University of Michigan and was intrigued. She announced to her family that she would sit on the sofa and not move until she had decided her life's mission.

She decided a career in medicine was the best way to help people. Her mother cried, and her father announced he wouldn't pay for her studies. Bertha remained strong in her dream. She would study medicine even if she had to work for every penny to pay for it.

While at the University of Michigan, Bertha met Mary McLean, an older medical student. Bertha admired Mary's enthusiastic commitment to medicine. Without her parents' financial support, Bertha needed to earn money for tuition, and when Mary offered her a job teaching calisthenics (which Bertha knew nothing about), she accepted.

After she graduated, Dr. Mary McLean waited an entire year before her first patient arrived. Bertha learned from Mary of the discrimination and lack of opportunity for women in medicine and how much work was needed before she would see success. But every day Mary took Bertha to the clinic to learn. After all she'd seen on the farm, Bertha *thought* she was well prepared to witness the gruesomeness of medicine.

One day in the surgical amphitheater, she watched the intern push a probe deep into a patient's wound and felt the room begin to spin. A wobbly Bertha fainted, and Mary escorted her home to recover. Bertha vowed she wouldn't faint the next time. But once again her knees buckled and down she went.

Finally, Bertha said,

> I am not only going, but I am going to stay until I faint, and when I come to, I am going to remain, no matter how many times I faint. We took front seats as usual, and sure enough, as soon as the curtain moved, and the table came nosing its way into the student side of the partition, I became ghastly faint.
>
> Dr. McLean reached for my hand. "Come!" she insisted.
>
> I shook my head.
>
> "Come!" she repeated.
>
> I shook my head until the hairpins loosened my hair, like Lady Godiva's, threatened to cover my shame.
>
> She urged, "Do come."
>
> I turned towards her, and said doggedly, "No!" and at this word all my faintness vanished, never to return at any time.

Bertha graduated from medical school in 1888 and took up clinical residencies at the Women's Hospital in Detroit, the Kalamazoo State Hospital for the Insane, and the New England Hospital for Women and Children in Boston. After four years of experience, she declared herself ready for practice, settling in Chicago, not knowing a single soul.

Bertha's practice began slowly. She worked as an unpaid anatomy instructor at the Woman's Medical School at Northwestern University and gave lectures on public health. As she waited for her first patient, Bertha received an emergency call to come at once to an apartment at 36th and Cottage Grove Avenue. She dressed quickly and, without a horse and buggy, hopped on the streetcar.

Dr. Rachel Hickey Carr greeted her and asked if she had been excited to attend her first real emergency. Bertha said yes, and Rachel was happy to give her that thrill. But there wasn't a real emergency; Rachel had tricked her. Instead the doctor offered her three days' work at the Columbian World's Fair in Chicago. The salary sustained her for one month!

Bertha generally wasn't afraid on her many late-night calls. Once, though, after being awakened at four in the morning by a teenaged boy in a broken-down buggy, she questioned whether she should go. Her neighbor pleaded with her to stay home and repeated the story of a doctor who had been murdered after taking a similar emergency in the dangerous part of town.

She told the neighbor she must go but to call the police if she didn't return in a few hours. The boy drove her down unfamiliar streets, increasing her fear. He instructed her to walk two houses down and climb the back staircase.

She was greeted by a man holding a baby in convulsions and two women kneeling before a picture of the Virgin Mary. "My fear was transformed into action." The baby's temperature had risen to a near-fatal 107 degrees. She stripped the baby and bathed it in ice-cold water. Afterward when the baby's temperature dropped to 101 degrees, it opened its eyes, and whispered "papa." Bertha never again suspected foul play on her late-night calls.

Slowly Bertha's practice grew, and by the time she moved in with her sister's family, her practice was booming. She treated mostly women and never knew when or if she would be paid. Her basement office consisted of an examining room (which was also her bedroom), a small waiting room, and a laboratory placed in the kitchen.

Bertha was determined to become an independent surgeon so she didn't have to discuss every operation with male doctors.

Bertha Van Hoosen, 1948. *Rochester Hills Museum at Van Hoosen Farm*

She operated in the hospital and saw patients in her office. She realized she had to stand alone when she failed; why not get the credit for every success? Once one of her surgical patients became infected when the nurses did not properly sterilize the equipment. When the woman was finally well enough to go home, Bertha presented her husband with a large bill. He was disgusted when told that before his wife could go home, he must pay the bill. The man replied that she could keep his wife. Bertha waived her fee and the man took his wife home. After that incident Bertha sterilized her own equipment the night before every surgery.

Alice's husband died and Bertha took over the family finances for herself, Alice, and Alice's daughter, Sarah. From that moment on, Bertha considered herself Sarah's "father," and the three of them formed an unbreakable family unit.

To make more money, Bertha became a traveling surgeon, operating in small midwestern towns and leaving her patients soon after surgery. She adopted a practice of standardized surgery that she had learned at the Mayo Clinic. The Mayo brothers, John and Charles, never used more than three kinds of surgical needles and limited their suture material. The nurses then knew what to expect and had few complications.

In 1912 Bertha sat for the civil service examination to be head of gynecological staff at Cook County Hospital in Chicago. Bertha knew she was qualified but wanted to know how well she would compete against the 300 male physicians. When she achieved the highest score, she refused to believe the good news until she had received official notification.

Her joy didn't last long; for the civil service examiners told her a mistake had been made. She hadn't achieved the highest score, the examiners said, a foreign-born male physician had. It was common at the time to award the job to a male, and since this physician was a foreigner, the board did not want to appear prejudiced against him, they said. But Bertha was convinced the board was prejudiced against *her* because she was a woman.

When she arrived home, she couldn't eat or sleep. The next day she raced over and demanded to know the birthplace of the doctor who had scored higher on the exam. Did he deserve the job she so desperately wanted?

TWILIGHT SLEEP

A German doctor, Dr. Karl Gauss, discovered "twilight sleep." When a woman in labor was given an injection of scopolamine-morphine, she had no pain or memory of the birth. An article published in June 1914 touting the miracle discovery caused wealthy American women to rush to Germany for this peaceful birth.

Feminists believed twilight sleep was a way to fight male domination, and its use became synonymous with women's rights. Dr. Bertha Van Hoosen wrote several papers on its use and by 1908 had used it in 2,000 healthy births. Many other physicians questioned the safety of twilight sleep because not all women fell asleep peacefully. Often the patient had to be restrained to keep from fighting the doctors and nurses. Dr. Van Hoosen invented a crib-like bed to keep patients from climbing out and escaping while under the drug's influence.

The use of twilight sleep fell off sharply when Francis Carmody died giving birth to her third child in 1915. Before the advent of twilight sleep, many women gave birth at home under the care of midwives and nurses. Hospitals soon became the place to go, awarding a new status to the obstetricians. Even as late as the 1970s, women were put to sleep to give birth using different drugs, with the doctors using forceps to deliver the baby.

But Bertha was forced to wait nearly a month to find out whether she had been given the job. The foreign doctor who had supposedly beaten her score had not in fact done so, nor did he have the naturalization papers necessary for him to work in the United States. Bertha claimed her rightful position. She walked into the warden's office of Cook County Hospital and asked to be shown to the women's surgical ward. He asked who she was, and when she told him the warden accused her of coming to work with a chip on her shoulder. She knew instead she had a woodpile on her shoulder but didn't say so and only told him in a firm voice that she was there to begin work.

Bertha continued to speak out to the medical community on its treatment of women. The American Medical Association had been established in 1870, and the few women who had been admitted faced isolation. In 1915 Bertha arranged a meeting of the medical women in Chicago, where she helped to found the American Medical Women's Association. Bertha became the group's first president.

In 1918 one of her former interns, Dr. Louis Moorehead, asked her to serve as acting head and professor of obstetrics at Loyola University in Chicago. Bertha was thrilled when the American Medical Association awarded an A grade to Loyola and shocked when they suggested that a man be placed at the head of the obstetrics department.

Bertha didn't want the school to suffer because she was a woman. When Father John Furay finally told her that *she* had been named the head of obstetrics, he said how much he appreciated the work she had done. He admitted to her the prejudice most male physicians held against women but told her the Loyola University administrators were prejudiced *for* her, not against.

Bertha held the position from 1918 to 1937, training more than 20 women in medicine. Called her "surgical daughters," the students found Bertha an arduous but inspiring teacher. Bertha also traveled to China to visit female medical missionaries there.

Her sister, Alice, broke her hip in 1950, and Bertha knew her place was with her beloved sister at the farm. There she wrote many letters and treated a few patients. Bertha suffered a stroke in 1952 and died at the age of 88.

The Petticoat Surgeon wrote late in life how she wished to be remembered, "When I was born, the door that separates the sexes had opened scarcely more than a crack. And it has been my privilege, my pain, and my pleasure to pound on that door, strain at its hinges and finally to see it, although not wide open, stand ajar."

LEARN MORE

Petticoat Surgeon by Bertha Van Hoosen (Pellegrini and Cudahy, 1947)

Susan La Flesche Picotte

A Bridge Between Worlds

It has always been a desire of mine to study medicine ever since I was a small girl for even then I saw the needs of my people for a good physician.

In 1883 18-year-old Susan La Flesche stayed by Alice's bedside for weeks. Alice Cunningham Fletcher visited the Omaha Indian Reservation several times as an ethnologist to study its customs and rituals and had become very close to Susan's older sisters Susette and Rosalie. During her 1883 visit, Alice became very ill.

Susan gave Alice pain medications. She bathed and fed her, nursing her back to health. Susan's success started her thinking. She remembered as a young child watching the white government doctor treat her people, sometimes successfully, sometimes not. The Omaha people had long suffered with new diseases introduced by white settlers. Sixty-five years before

Susan La Flesche Picotte.
National Anthropological Archives, Smithsonian Institution

Susan was born, the smallpox outbreak of 1800–1801 reduced the Omaha population by more than half. In addition as more American fur traders moved to the Missouri Valley, the Omahas became increasingly dependent on the white traders. Susan asked herself what she could do to help her people.

Susan La Flesche was born in a tepee on the plains of Nebraska in 1865. The Native American world she was born into was changing, and her father, Joseph (Chief Iron Eye) La Flesche, believed they would have to adapt to white people's ways to survive. But he didn't want to give up on tradition or speak out against the Omahas who did wish to adopt new ways. So Joseph chose to bridge the differences. He was the son of a French fur trader and a Ponca woman and was adopted by the Omaha Tribe as an adult when he married an Omaha woman. Chief Joseph was the last chief of the Omaha Tribe. Susan's mother, Mary Gale, was the daughter of US Army physician John Gale and his Omaha wife, Nicomi.

Susan's family moved from the tepee to a wood frame house overlooking the Missouri River. Joseph farmed the reservation land, and the family planted beans and corn in the rich soil. He tried to preserve their Omaha culture yet would not allow the

THE TREATY OF 1854

The Treaty of 1854 changed the life of the Omaha Indians. They ceded almost six million acres of land to the United States and were moved to a 300,000-acre reservation in northeastern Nebraska. In exchange for the land, the government promised the Omaha $40,000 a year for the next 30 years. Traders and agents assigned to the reservation created many loopholes designed to cheat the Omahas out of their expected payments. Many were left to fend for themselves, some surviving on little more than roots. By 1855 the Omaha Indian population dipped drastically once more, this time to around 800.

When pioneers began to arrive in great numbers, the buffalo population also fell. The US government wanted the Native American land for westward expansion. One way to push the Native Americans to the reservations was to take away their food supply by destroying the buffalo population. This slaughter, along with little effort by the government to enforce treaty obligations stopping settlers from killing for sport and hides, as well as other environmental problems, dropped the buffalo population almost to extinction. The Omaha were forced to change their way of life because they could no longer hunt buffalo for their food and clothing needs. There were approximately 50 million buffalo in 1850; by the 1880s only a few hundred remained. To survive, the Omaha Tribe learned to farm along the Missouri River.

traditional Omaha tattoos to be placed on his daughters, nor did he give the three youngest girls Omaha names. His children must be accepted in both worlds, he reasoned.

Susan and her older sisters, Susette, Rosalie, and Marguerite, and her brother, Francis, learned to read and write in English. Through play and repetition, Susan also learned the importance of work in belonging to the tribe. She wrote later in life on the chore of collecting water, "It was a weary toilsome walk, clear down to the spring and back under the hot sun, through the stubble, barefooted and we were happy little mortals when our dreaded work was finished."

Susan's father, Joseph, knew that education was the key to the Native Americans' survival, for only then could they compete with the Euro-Americans. Through her father's fights against the sale of alcohol to the Native Americans and to ensure the government kept its bargain of making annual payments to displaced people, young Susan absorbed her father's courage. After learning as much as they could from the Presbyterians' limestone mission school and later from the Quakers, Susan and Marguerite were sent east to Elizabeth, New Jersey, for high school. Susan's oldest sister, Susette, had already graduated from high school, while Rosalie finished her education at the local school.

After three years studying math, writing, reading, and English, Susan returned to the reservation. She was thrilled to return to her pony. As she rode across the Nebraska hills, she witnessed her people struggle mightily, barely eking out a living. She wondered what she could do to help them.

Susan's parents and grandmother did not want to send her away again, but in the fall of 1884, Susan and Marguerite traveled to Virginia to attend the Hampton Normal and Agriculture Institute. The coeducational college was founded to educate newly freed slaves and Native Americans. Susan's grandmother worried whether she would be adequately chaperoned while she studied with boys.

At the graduation ceremony a few years later, Susan gave the salutatorian speech. She thanked her benefactors for supporting her financially, saying, "Indians are only beginning; so do not try to put us down, but help us to climb higher."

Her application to the Woman's Medical College of Philadelphia had been accepted, but without any money she didn't think she would be able to attend. Remembering the excellent care she had received from Susan, Alice Fletcher connected her with Sara Kinney, president of the Connecticut Indian Association. The organization looked for young Native American women interested in advanced education and agreed to pay Susan's way through medical school. In a letter to Mrs. Kinney, Susan later wrote, "I can do a great deal more than as a mere teacher, for the home is the foundation of all things for the Indians, and my work I hope will be chiefly in the homes of my people."

A nervous Susan La Flesche stepped off the train in Philadelphia. She had had Marguerite with her when she attended both Elizabeth Institute and Hampton. Now she began medical school alone. At Hampton she had studied with other Native American girls, and now white girls surrounded her. She worried they would be more educated. Would she be able to keep up?

Susan wanted to belong, but she compared her plain calico dresses to her new roommate's dresses made of lace and silk. Over time she shopped for clothes like her fellow students and attended as many social events as possible. She was exposed to different religions and noted the grand music of the Catholic Mass.

In the end Susan realized she was there to become a doctor so she could help her people. Her studies must come first. Her lectures consisted of obstetrics, anatomy, physiology, chemistry, and histology (cell anatomy). She also observed clinics and dissected cadavers. Girls were expected to be faint at such sights, but Susan wrote in a letter to her sister Rosalie that it was "interesting to get all the arteries and the branches . . . everything has a name from the little tiny holes to the bones. It is splendid."

While Susan was studying to become a doctor, Rosalie had stayed on the reservation to take care of their mother and father. Susan felt guilty and did what she could from far away, sending letters full of medical advice. She told Rosalie to rest when she was pregnant, not to lift heavy objects, and to try to enjoy her children. For a sore on her mother's hand, she sent a packet of castile soap and some carbolated (antiseptic) Vaseline to cure it.

Good nutrition leading to good health was a new idea for the 1880s. When Dr. Sue, as she called herself, came into extra cash, she sent it home for her family to purchase meat, chicken, and other nutritious food not easily obtained. Preventative medicine was just beginning to catch on.

On March 14, 1889, Susan graduated from medical school along with 35 other students. She was praised for her "courage, constancy, and ability" by the professors. To further her studies, Susan secured a coveted spot as an assistant to the resident physician at the Woman's Hospital of Philadelphia.

During her internship Susan traveled with the resident physician on house calls. The poverty-stricken neighborhoods reminded her of home and her promise to make life better on the Omaha reservation.

She returned to the reservation as the Omaha Indian School physician and found the school in horrible condition. She set about cleaning the rooms, encouraging better sanitation, and providing more nutritious food. After a few months, the Indian agent Robert Ashley gave her a glowing report and stated there was "not a child in bed on account of sickness," and Frank Armstrong from the Office of Indian Affairs said that she was "a good influence with the pupils." And at night Susan taught the children English and arithmetic.

But Susan wanted to do more than serve the Omaha children. She had succeeded with the schoolchildren, and word of her success spread throughout the reservation. The Omaha people trusted her because she spoke their language and understood their customs. When she was hired as the reservation's doctor, Susan told Sara Kinney, the woman who had funded her training, "My office hours are any and all hours of the day and night." Susan treated one young child and worried all night whether she had made the correct diagnosis, so the next day she rode the eight miles to his home. There she found him playing happily in the creek. He recovered so quickly that soon she found herself swamped with many new patients.

Roads were rough on the reservation, and Susan was responsible for 1,244 patients. Most days she could only visit 10 to 12 patients as their homes were spread out over 30 miles. But Susan was the reservation's only trained medical doctor, and she vowed to help them as best she could, even through the long, frigid winters. She wore a thick coat to block the biting wind as she took off in her buggy through the heavy snow. She treated more than 600 patients during the influenza outbreak of 1891–1892, sometimes at temperatures as low as 20 below 0. Each night when she arrived home, she placed a lantern in her window so patients could find her.

After four exhausting years as the reservation's only physician, Susan decided to resign. She suffered from earaches and neck and back pain, and the long hours in the cold buggy over rough roads had taken their toll. She also felt a strong responsibility to take care of her ill mother.

Susan (left), her sister Marguerite, and their husbands, Henry Picotte (seated) and Walter Diddock (standing). *National Anthropological Archives, Smithsonian Institution*

Susan had long said she would remain single to serve her people, but in 1894 she married Henry Picotte. Henry was a Dakota Indian from the Yankton Sioux Tribe and the brother of her sister Marguerite's late husband, Charles. Susan gave birth to sons Caryl, in 1895, and Pierre, in 1898. Henry farmed Susan's land allotment while she cared for their sons and returned to her medical practice. But her health failed again, and suddenly everyone feared for her life. Friends and family came to her side bringing food and good wishes. She felt truly appreciated for the first time and wrote, "This summer taught me a lesson I hope I never forget."

Alcohol abuse had led to deserted farms, street brawls, and extreme poverty and had ruined many lives on the Omaha reservation. Susan was determined to do something about it. In her house calls, she included lectures on the danger of drinking, and she fought against the whites who sold alcohol to her tribe. But she had no magic cure for those who drank. In fact, in 1905 her husband, Henry, died of complications related to alcoholism. Heartbroken, Susan moved with her two young sons to Macy, Nebraska, to start again.

Since the days of traveling the reservation in her buggy, Susan had dreamed of building a hospital where she could care for her patients. She worked tirelessly to facilitate fund-raising, and finally in 1913 the Walthill Hospital opened with 12 beds, a maternity ward, and an operating room.

Susan's influence over the Omaha Tribe was widespread. Not only did she become the first degreed Native American woman physician, she also served as her tribe's advisor, missionary, teacher, and cultural bridge to the white world. She died at the young age of 50 on September 18, 1915, from the degenerative bone disease she had suffered from for years. She did as her father had asked by helping her people transition from Native American ways to white society's ways while still preserving their Omaha culture. She was remembered for the care and love she offered her people.

LEARN MORE

Homeward the Arrow's Flight: The Story of Susan La Flesche by Marion Marsh Brown (Field Mouse Productions, 1980)

Into a New Country: Eight Remarkable Women of the West by Liza Ketchum (Little, Brown, 2000)

Native American Doctor: The Story of Susan La Flesche Picotte by Jeri Ferris (Carolrhoda Books, 1991)

Elizabeth Kenny

Dogged Nurse from the Outback

It is better to be a lion for a day than a sheep all your life.

Elizabeth straddled her horse and spurred him to action. The loose saddle wobbled as she cantered through the bush country. Suddenly Elizabeth was thrown from the horse, landing hard on her wrist. But when Elizabeth cried, it was not from the pain but because the horse had gotten the best of her. Her father whisked her away in a buggy 40 miles to Toowoomba, where the closest doctor practiced.

Her broken wrist required extra care and Dr. Aeneas McDonnell provided it, taking a liking to this brash daughter of Irish descent. He took Elizabeth into his own home to recover, and that's where Elizabeth Kenny's love of the human body began. Each afternoon she poured over the medical books in Aeneas's study and played with the skeleton hanging in the corner.

Elizabeth Kenny was born in New South Wales, Australia, just outside the village of Warialda on September 20, 1880. Girls were not supposed to be brassy, opinionated, or stubborn, but Elizabeth was all of these. In fact her mother, Mary, called her the "wild one" because she was always riding bareback through the bush.

When a depression hit New South Wales in the 1890s, the Kenny family moved north to the warmth of Queensland. They settled on a ranch called Heddington Hill, where Elizabeth's father took charge of the farm's horses.

Elizabeth's young brother Bill had been sickly his entire life. His muscles were so weak that he had to be carried piggyback through the rough bush country to school. One day Elizabeth rigged up a model of the human body in the barn using a skeleton borrowed from Aeneas. She used colored ribbons to identify muscles and attached them to pulleys. One pull of the rope and the model moved, showing her the muscle's function. She sent away for *Sandow's System*, a book on bodybuilding, and together she and Bill designed a way to strengthen his physique.

Elizabeth wanted to help others by becoming a missionary in Africa. Aeneas suggested she learn nursing, and she later decided the Australian people needed her instead. No one knows whether, or if, Elizabeth completed nurse's training. Most likely she learned through on-the-job training.

Elizabeth ordered a red cape and nurse's uniform and declared that she was open for business. As soon as she heard of a sick child, she galloped away with her packed bag. One day in 1911, a frantic farmer named McNeil called out for help. Elizabeth raced to the family on horseback. She found two-year-old Amy wailing in terrific pain. Her legs and arms were twisted and tight. Any attempt by Elizabeth to examine the child or straighten her tangled legs led to more pain. Elizabeth had never seen this illness before.

She spurred her horse Thunderbolt and galloped away to send a telegram to Aeneas. She waited for a response. At long last his bleak answer was received: "Infantile Paralysis. Polio. Nothing to be done. Do the best you can with symptoms presenting themselves."

Elizabeth prayed as she rode off into the cold and windy winter night. She thought about the girl's symptoms.

> I knew the relaxing power of heat. I filled a frying pan with salt, placed it over the fire, then poured it into a bag and applied it to the leg that was giving the most pain. After an anxious wait, I saw no relief followed the application. I then prepared a linseed meal poultice, but the weight of this seemed only to increase the pain. At last I tore a blanket made from soft Australian wool into suitable strips and wrung them out in boiling water. These I wrapped gently about the poor tortured muscles. The whimpering of the child ceased almost immediately, and after a few more applications her eyes closed slowly and she fell asleep.

When Amy awoke she cried out, "I want them rags that wells my legs." Amy's legs improved after several treatments, and Elizabeth began to exercise them. She called this process reeducation because she believed polio caused the pathway between the muscles and the brain to be broken, causing the paralysis. The patient concentrating on moving that muscle helped to reopen the pathway.

Many people suspected Elizabeth made up this story to spread the news of her treatment's success. Aeneas found out she had treated many others this way and said, "The way before you is going to be hard. . . . But if you have the courage to carry on, a great reward will be yours. The great cities of the [E]arth will bid you welcome."

The traditional polio treatment was to seal the patient's body in heavy plaster casts or braces. Doctors believed that this forced

POLIO

Poliomyelitis, or infantile paralysis, is an ancient disease with major epidemics largely unknown before the 20th century. Polio is a relatively mild virus, and because patients were often unaware they had the disease, it spread easily.

Paralytic polio began to appear in the United States around 1900. In 1916, centered in New York City, there were more than 27,000 cases, causing 6,000 deaths. At that time it wasn't clear how the virus spread, leading to many mandatory quarantines. Swimming pools, camps, and state fairs were off limits, as no one wanted to be exposed to the disease.

Widespread terror gripped the United States during the polio outbreaks of the 1940s and '50s. The worst epidemic occurred in 1952, fueling a great push for a working vaccine. Doctors Jonas Salk and Albert Sabin each came out with promising vaccines, and in 1955 immunizations began, signaling the end of polio in the United States. Eventually it was Albert Sabin's live poliovirus vaccine that provided stronger immunity. The United States has been polio free since 1979, although in underdeveloped countries without the vaccine, polio is still a threat today.

the patient to rest and avoid crippled limbs. They didn't believe that Elizabeth's hot packs could work.

Elizabeth opened a small nursing clinic outside Brisbane, Australia, where she delivered babies and treated accident victims and sickness, including new polio cases. But each polio case was different, and she couldn't help everyone. Many children never walked again, and many died.

Doubting doctors questioned her. Could this young Australian nurse with so little education be smarter than they were? She had two strikes against her: she was an untrained bush nurse and a woman. But stubborn Elizabeth believed in her treatment while the doctors belittled her.

In 1914 when Elizabeth wanted to serve in World War I, Aeneas wrote to the Australian government, saying that her years of nursing in the bush qualified her for service. The Australian Army Nursing Service gave her the title of "sister," which had nothing to do with religion, instead meaning "senior nurse." She became known as Sister Kenny.

During the war darkened ships with all of the lights switched off to prevent enemy attacks transported the Australian wounded home. Elizabeth made 12 trips from Europe to Australia during three years. The war ended and Elizabeth was exhausted. At her checkup she heard the doctors say she was coming to the end of her journey. She said to the doctors, "If I have only six months to live, then I'd better get busy."

She had been diagnosed with a weak heart, and after resting in Europe for several months, Elizabeth picked up where she left off caring for sick children. The doctors had given up on one child named Daphne, who had cerebral palsy. A form of brain damage that occurs before, during, or after birth, cerebral palsy affects both muscle control and coordination. Elizabeth thought she could help Daphne by bringing her home for constant treatment. She exercised Daphne's limbs and filled the hot tub for long soaks. She said later, "Although my special life's work had not yet really begun, I always think of this period as the starting point."

In 1933 Mr. Charles Chuter arranged for Elizabeth to present her polio treatment at Brisbane General Hospital. Smart and successful doctors packed the room, and this was her chance to prove her treatment. But she stumbled over the presentation. Elizabeth used words like *spasm* and *reeducation*, words the doctors would never use. Even though she claimed her methods worked, she had no proof. The doctors turned away, calling her a quack nurse from the outback.

For many years crippled children came to her from far away. Please help them, their parents begged. Elizabeth straightened her six-foot frame in a powerful stance against the doctors and their old treatments. She ripped off plaster casts and discarded metal braces. She knew she was right, but the doubting doctors gathered to write a report that said Elizabeth's methods hurt her patients. Crushed, she decided to go to America to explain her treatment. She later recalled, "Although I was well into my fifties and comfortably settled in my own establishment . . . I had already traveled much and was now content to enjoy the untroubled peace of my own home. But whatever that Power is that guides our destinies, it had a different plan for me, and I felt obliged to follow it."

In April 1940 Elizabeth, along with her daughter, Mary, whom she had adopted in 1926, stepped off the dock in Los Angeles, California. Elizabeth sported her signature large black hat, mustering her confidence. Perhaps America would be a new beginning to her long-waged battle. But the doctors in New York and Chicago sent her away. They called her rude and stubborn and said she was difficult to get along with. For more than 30 years, she had battled medical men. Her hair had turned white, and at 60 years old she was on the verge of giving up. Would her dogged nature let her?

An Australian doctor had suggested she visit the famous Mayo Clinic in Rochester, Minnesota. They didn't have any polio patients, but two hours away in Minneapolis, young children filled the polio wards. Elizabeth decided to give it one last try. Drs. Wallace Cole and Miland Knapp watched Elizabeth work and saw improvements in her patients. Dr. Miland Knapp asked her to examine a young boy whose progress had stalled. She removed the splint on his arm and began treatment. Because his arm had been confined in the splint, his muscles had shortened. The treatment relaxed his muscles and then Elizabeth began the reeducation of his arm. Soon he was back

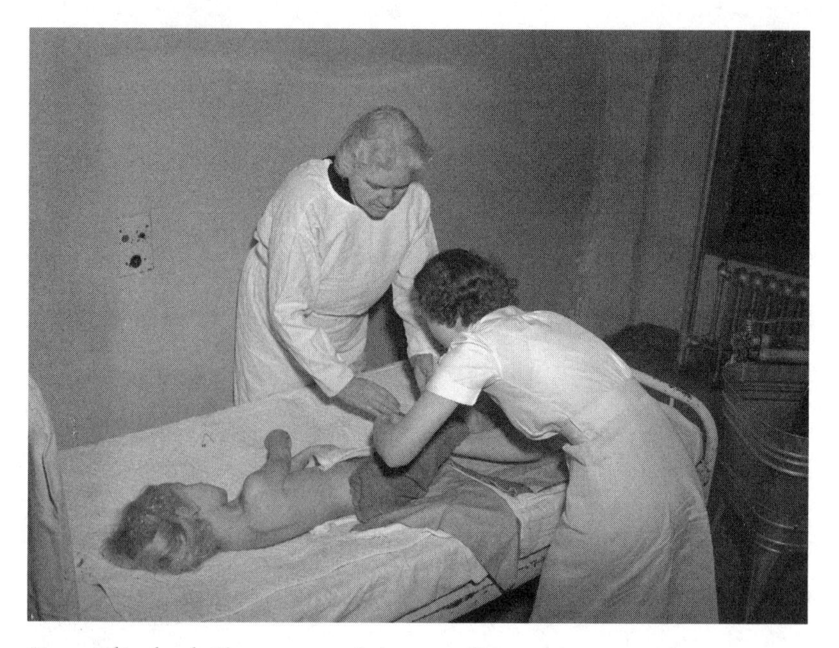

Sister Elizabeth Kenny examining a polio patient, 1945. *Minnesota Historical Society*

to shoveling snow in the driveway. The Minnesota doctors gave her a cautious thumbs-up. She carried on with new energy.

The National Foundation for Infantile Paralysis (NFIP), later renamed the March of Dimes, concluded that Elizabeth's treatment greatly helped her patients. It was what she had been fighting for all these years. She dared not rest! She crisscrossed the country training new nurses, who she insisted dress in pale blue to identify them as Kenny technicians. The Kenny technicians

Sister Kenny aboard the *Queen Mary*, 1950. *Wikimedia Commons*

admired the courageous nurse who challenged the medical establishment.

One of Elizabeth's patients, Henry Haverstock, recalled her later. "She wasn't a quitter. When she got her teeth on into something she hung, stuck on. I don't think there is another woman in the world who could come over here at age 60 and try to get acceptance for something she was fighting all her life for in Australia."

In December 1942 the Elizabeth Kenny Institute opened its doors in Minneapolis. The institute still exists today, having been renamed Courage Kenny. It now focuses on accident and stroke rehabilitation. The American public adored Elizabeth, and she loved the limelight. A writer from the *New York Post* said of her, "There are power in her long arms, courage in her convictions and a tart edge to her tongue."

She became so popular that the Gallup Poll found her to be one of the most influential women in America for nine years running. One year she even beat out First Lady Eleanor Roosevelt!

Elizabeth sailed home to Australia in 1951 and died shortly after on November 30, 1952, not living to see the polio vaccine's success.

LEARN MORE

And They Shall Walk: The Life Story of Sister Elizabeth Kenny by Elizabeth Kenny (Dodd, Mead, 1943)

Healing Warrior: A Story About Sister Elizabeth Kenny by Emily Crofford (Carolrhoda Books, 1989)

More than Petticoats: Remarkable Minnesota Women by Bonnye E. Stuart (TwoDot Press, 2004)

Mary Carson Breckinridge

Mountaineer Nurse on Horseback

Winter had set in early with heavy snows. . . . We came onto a mountain so steep and so heavily timbered that it was impossible to ride down it. So, Teddy Bear [Mary's horse] and I just sat down on our haunches and slid. . . . Our guardian angels need skis to keep up with us at times, now as then.

When 24-year-old Mary Breckinridge became a widow after just one year of marriage, she wondered what to do with her life. She had had a privileged but sparse education that had left her untrained for any means of supporting herself. What was she fit for?

A friend had founded a girls' school named Banner's Elk in the mountains of North Carolina. Mary thought she might help. But the school didn't have a need for her, and she left after only a few days, checking into a little hotel in the valley. But there in

Mary Breckinridge feeding Babbette. *Frontier Nursing Service*

the valley one small boy had been stricken with typhoid fever. His mother sat by helplessly. As Mary comforted the little boy, it occurred to her that if she trained as a nurse, she could be of use to children.

Mary Carson Breckinridge was born on February 17, 1881, in Memphis, Tennessee. Her aristocratic family shaped her early life. She was the daughter of the US ambassador to Russia and the granddaughter of the vice president of the United States under James Buchanan. She traveled widely with her family from St. Petersburg, Russia, where her ambassador father was stationed, to boarding school in the mountains of Switzerland. With a family home in Kentucky and another house in Canada, young Mary was at ease riding bareback through the wilderness.

In 1907, two years after her husband's death, she enrolled in nurse's training at St. Luke's Hospital School of Nursing in New York. Her studies were tiring but rewarding. The nurses reported to duty at seven o'clock in the morning and set up the operating rooms. The surgeons operated all day, and when they were finished the student nurses were responsible for cleaning up while the graduate nurses went off duty.

While working in the nursery, Mary came upon a baby named Margaret who was born with a severe case of spina bifida. Margaret's mother had abandoned her. Spina bifida is a birth defect where the spinal column does not close all the way. Today about 90 percent of babies born with this defect live to be adults, and 80 percent have normal intelligence, according to the Spina Bifida Association.

Mary described Margaret: "Her eyes were luminous. . . . During the weeks I attended her, she became dear to me. . . . Although this baby was crippled for life, the feeling that I had for her was not one of pity. . . . Margaret and I had become friends. I wanted her companionship, and I wanted to make life easy for her as long as she lived."

A mix-up occurred as Mary tried to take the discharged baby from the Lying-In Hospital (a hospital for treating maternity patients and their babies) back to St. Luke's. She had to go before a board to explain why she had "stolen" a baby! Mary was cleared of wrongdoing. The district supervisor knew she was trying to do a good deed. Two days later Margaret died. Mary took charge of her body and saw that she had a respectable burial and grave.

After receiving her nursing degree in 1910, 26-year-old Mary returned home to nurse her sick mother. She remarried in 1912 and had two children. First was "Breckie," born Clifford Breckinridge Thompson, in 1914, and Polly, born prematurely, in 1916. Polly lived for only six hours. After Polly's death Mary said, "The more we seek to hold our children to ourselves, the less they are ours."

Breckie was a lively, fair-haired boy who adored the outdoors, and Mary set out to give him as many outdoor experiences as possible. When Breckie was just four years old, tragedy struck again. He died of appendicitis after a swift illness. Mary had suffered through the death of two children. She divorced her husband (unusual for the time) and promised herself she would never love anyone, and would never allow love from anyone else, for the rest of her life.

Mary searched for another purpose. World War I had just ended, and France suffered greatly at the hands of the Germans. She joined the American Committee for Devastated France and got permission to help the children in as many villages as possible.

Mary wrote to her mother describing the desperate times. "Well, the Duvauchelle family had nothing left but the worn clothes they wore. We have given them bedding, clothes, groceries. . . . If I could give right now a goat to every family that has a baby, I think we could go far to saving many that are dying. . . . I wish I had a thousand goats right now. I wish I had fifty."

Mary's mother organized a letter-writing campaign and money poured in. "They came in carload lots from the Pyrenees, each car with its own goatherd to feed and milk them on the long trip across France. . . . As I opened the door I heard a 'Baa, maa, baa,' and there stood a white goat."

Mary wanted to help the poor in rural America, too. She began by surveying the needs of the people. Throughout the summer of 1923, she rode more than 650 miles around creeks, through valleys, and up the mountains of Kentucky. What kind of help did the residents need? Could Mary help them?

She had learned of the nurse-midwives in France and in 1924 studied midwifery in England. Her goal was to provide the same type of nursing and midwifery services she had witnessed in France.

As Mary rode through the Kentucky woods on the way to noon dinner with the locals, she discovered land like no other. "I rode down Muncy Creek, forded the Middle Fork and rode slowly along its banks. . . . When I raised my eyes to towering forest trees, and then let them fall on a cleared place where one might have a garden, when I passed some jutting rocks, I fell in love. To myself and my horse I said, 'Someday I'm going to build me a log house right there.'"

Mary's plans for the nursing service were coming together in 1925. She had gathered local people of power as well as a few nurses. She set up regional committees and seeded the pot with her own money. It was enough to last for the first three years of the Frontier Nursing Service.

The first nurse's station was set up in Hyden, Kentucky. One by one Mary established six centers and assigned two nurse-midwives to each one. Each hub served about 250 families and followed the waterways of the Middle Fork of the Kentucky and the Red Bird Rivers.

Mary built her home on the land she had seen two years earlier. Her aunt Jane named it Wendover, meaning restful and inviting place. It was known as the "big house" and also served as the Frontier Nursing Service headquarters. Even though the seven-room center was without indoor plumbing, Mary called it an oasis of modern science, which it was compared to the surrounding primitive buildings.

The service got off to a bright start, with 561 visits in the first quarter. But one of the biggest problems in the early operation was the lack of communication. Telephone service had not yet come to the Kentucky wilderness, so Mary hired volunteers to act as couriers, carrying both information and supplies. Young women anxious for adventure mounted horses to guide visitors and patients alike through the wilderness, taking seven days to travel to all the stations.

Trains carried supplies that were then transferred to horse-drawn wagons and, in times of high water, flat-bed boats whooshing down the flooded creeks. To ease the need for outside supplies, chicken houses were built at each outpost. Nurses and patients alike planted gardens each spring and canned vegetables for the winter.

Mary built a 12-bed hospital at Hyden in 1928, and every donation thereafter allowed a few more beds and services to be added. The state-of-the-art hospital had electric lights and refrigeration and became the center of the Frontier Nursing Service. By 1929 the nursing service covered about 700 square miles, serving more than 10,000 patients.

Throughout the growth of the Frontier Nursing Service, Mary spent long days fund-raising away from the mountains.

Mary Breckinridge with Frontier Nursing Service's 10,000th baby, Marlene Wooten, 1954. *Frontier Nursing Service*

At first she was shy about speaking out and hesitated to ask for money, but her service could not survive without the much-needed funds.

The nurse-midwives gained the confidence of the local families as they checked in during weekly rides. Often they would have to transport the mother-to-be, "riding sideways, on the rump of the horse, behind the nurse-midwife. Where else in the world we often asked ourselves would such a woman be brought to a hospital door in such a fashion?"

One day, twins Enos and Eva were carried, one each by their father and older sister. Their mother had died of childbed fever, and their father asked the nurses to save his children. He knew that they'd need milk, so he brought his cow as well. Mary wrote in her autobiography, "We knew the minute we saw them, that the saving of their lives and the restoring of them to health would be a long, hard task. We kept them for a year . . . and when we sent them home they were magnificent specimens of babyhood . . . six teeth each, both were rosy and brown from sun baths, and both could stand alone."

Milk was always in demand, and one donated cow, named "October" after the month in which she arrived, provided six gallons of milk each day! When she died of pneumonia 12 years later, she was given an honorable burial.

Prevention was a primary goal of the Frontier Nursing Service. The nurses on horseback made frequent well-child and adult checkups and educated the families on good nutrition and hygiene. Donor support would come easier if Mary could prove her success with hard data, so nurses were required to keep meticulous records.

For 40 years Mary perfected her Frontier Nursing Service. She died in 1965 at the age of 84. Her work continues. A new hospital replaced the one she built, and her home in Wendover is on the National Register of Historic Places and is currently a bed-and-breakfast. The Frontier Nursing Service School of Midwifery and Family Nursing thrives, as do four rural health clinics. The nurses today ride in jeeps rather than on horses.

FRONTIER NURSING UNIVERSITY

Mary Breckinridge founded the Frontier Graduate School of Midwifery in 1939, just as World War II was beginning. Today the Frontier Nursing University (FNU) reaches many more people than Mary Breckinridge ever dreamed it would. FNU offers several degrees, including a doctor of nursing practice degree and a master of science in nursing degree with concentrations in family nurse practitioner, nurse-midwife, and women's health-care nurse practitioner. Students earn these degrees through web-based learning, and clinical experience is gained through hospitals and clinics in their own communities. Over the last 75 years, FNU has educated more than 4,000 midwives and nurses, and the nurse-midwifery program is rated number one in the United States according to *US News & World Report*.

LEARN MORE

Clever Country: Kentucky Mountain Trails by Caroline Gardner (Fleming H. Revell, 1931)

Frontier Nursing Service website, https://frontiernursing.org

Mary on Horseback: Three Mountain Stories by Rosemary Wells (Puffin Books, 1998)

Wide Neighborhoods: A Story of the Frontier Nursing Service by Mary Breckinridge (University Press of Kentucky, 1952)

Helen Taussig

From Blue to a Lovely Shade of Pink

A good research doctor has curiosity, persistence and a willingness to work hard. . . . You take a problem and mull it over until you see what can and needs to be done first and do that. Usually that opens up the next obvious thing to do, and you do that and continue until suddenly the problem is solved. You can't try to eat the whole cake at once or you'll choke on it.

Helen Taussig crouched over an oxygenated salt solution in Boston University's medical lab in 1923. She immersed strips of heart tissue from a cat's left ventricle into the solution. At first she thought she had imagined seeing muscle contractions, but after a few minutes in the cold, 32-degree-centigrade solution, the tissue moved again, just like the rhythmic contractions of a beating heart. Helen spent the next several months repeating the experiment using tissue from oxen, dogs, calves, and finally humans.

Satisfied that it wasn't a one-time event, she published a paper in the *American Journal of Physiology*. She hadn't even begun medical school.

Helen Brooke Taussig was born on May 24, 1898, in Cambridge, Massachusetts, to Edith and Frank Taussig. Knowledge and culture were more important than money in the Taussig family. Though they lived comfortably, education was the family's center stone. During the summer the family traveled to their beach house in Massachusetts, and even though the cool ocean water called to Helen and her three siblings, studies came first.

Most students could read a page or two aloud without making a mistake when the teacher called them to the front of the class. Helen never made it through a single paragraph. The letters jumped and twisted on the page and Helen couldn't make sense of what she saw. Her teachers thought that if she really wanted to read, she had the intelligence to do so. Perhaps she wasn't trying hard enough. But Helen had a language-processing disability called dyslexia, and because her teachers didn't understand it, they were unable to help her.

When Helen was nine, her happy life changed. Her mother had been diagnosed with tuberculosis and was sent to bed. The only treatment at the time was rest, fresh air, and healthy food. Her mother died two years later when Helen was only 11.

Frank Taussig, Helen's father, was an important man. As a professor of economics at Harvard, he was called the father of modern economics. He loved to teach and that extended to his children, especially Helen. Each day as she struggled to read, he sat nearby, coaching her through the words, sentences, paragraphs, and pages. He was patient and kind, although deep down he was concerned that Helen would not make it through elementary school.

DYSLEXIA

The National Institutes of Health defines dyslexia as a brain-based type of learning disability, which can be hereditary. People with dyslexia have trouble recognizing words they should know due to problems classifying speech sounds and learning how they relate to letters and words. Decoding, or understanding the meaning of words, and spelling are difficult as well. These problems often lead to poor reading comprehension and difficulty adding new words to a person's vocabulary. Those with dyslexia are not stupid or lazy, and although it is a lifelong disability, there are therapies that can help the student become a better reader.

Year by year her reading improved, and she preferred poetry because of the few words on each page. Because of her reading and health problems (a mild case of tuberculosis), Helen learned perseverance as one of life's great qualities.

After graduating from Cambridge School for Girls in 1917, Helen began college at Radcliffe, where her mother had studied biology and botany. But after two years at Radcliffe, Helen wasn't happy there. She talked her father into letting her go to the University of California at Berkeley, where she earned a bachelor of arts degree in 1921.

When she returned home, her father suggested a career in public health because he thought it was a better field for women than medicine. She applied to Harvard's School of Public Health and was told she could study there but that she would never be awarded a degree because she was a woman. She said, "Who is going to be such a fool as to spend four years studying and not get a degree?"

She decided instead on a medical degree and applied to Harvard Medical School to audit a histology course, meaning she could take the class without receiving credit. Harvard did not admit women to its medical school until 1945. She was forced to sit away from the male medical students so as not to "contaminate the male students." Helen next took a year's coursework in anatomy at Boston University. Dr. Alexander Begg suggested she study the heart muscle.

The next year Helen applied to Johns Hopkins Medical School in Baltimore and was accepted. Johns Hopkins had admitted women since its opening in 1893. When the original building fund began to run out of money, five wealthy women stepped in to help under the condition that women be admitted on the same terms as men. While in medical school, Helen continued her heart research and graduated in 1927. When Helen was not selected for the only internship given to women at Johns Hopkins, she was forced to try something else. Her professor of pediatrics said, "That which is a disappointment in time may prove to be one's good fortune."

Johns Hopkins School of Medicine appointed Dr. Edwards Park to head the pediatric department. Noting her work in heart research, Dr. Edwards Park named Helen the physician in charge of pediatric cardiology. Was it wise, she asked her father, to choose such a narrow specialization? He replied, "Helen, for a woman, recognition will only come through specialization."

Listening to patients' hearts was a critical part of the job. The stethoscope, along with other tools in the lab, required a keen sense of hearing. Helen came down with a serious case of whooping cough and noticed that the music she loved to listen to became fuzzy and then disappeared. She retained partial hearing but wondered how a cardiologist with a severe hearing loss could succeed.

Hearing aids of the day simply weren't good enough to allow one to hear the subtleties of a beating heart. One day Helen placed her hands on the chest of a child. She realized she could feel the pulse of the beating heart. She practiced by figuring out how lightly she could touch an object such as a chair next to a radio playing music and still feel the vibrations. Soon she was able to diagnose conditions that hearing doctors couldn't, even with the aid of a stethoscope. She learned to lip-read and eventually wore a boxy hearing aid.

But Helen was stressed coping with two disabilities. She left Baltimore, seeking solace in Cape Cod for the summer. Every morning, just as she had as a child, she dove into the cool ocean

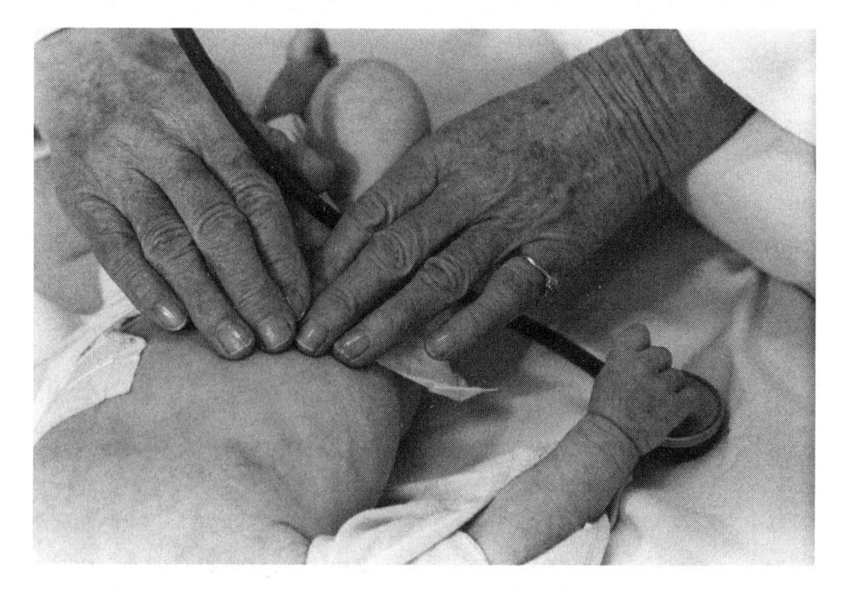

Helen Taussig using touch to feel a baby's heartbeat. *The Alan Mason Chesney Medical Archives of the Johns Hopkins Medical Institutions*

THE HEART

A normal heart is about the size of your fist if you're a child and about two fists if you're an adult. It has four chambers and four valves, each with a specific purpose. The right atrium receives oxygen-poor blood after its journey through the body and sends it into the right ventricle. From there the blood is pumped to the lungs to receive much-needed oxygen. This oxygenated blood is then sent to the left atrium, where it flows to the left ventricle. Finally the left ventricle pumps the oxygenated blood out to the entire body.

This is a continuous process, beginning before we are born and lasting until death. The average heart beats 100,000 times a day and 35 million times in a year. The heart will beat more than 2.5 billion times in an average lifetime.

waters. In the fall Helen returned to Baltimore to care for the children at Johns Hopkins Heart Clinic, working in the Harriet Lane Home for Invalid Children.

There she saw children with congenital heart defects, as well as those with rheumatic fever caused by bacteria called streptococci, or strep. These often-deadly bacteria caused damage to the heart, and cases didn't diminish until the discovery of penicillin. Would Helen ever be able to help all these poor children?

The cases where children had congenital (from birth) heart defects were her biggest concern; Helen often called these cases the "crossword puzzles of Harriet Lane." Operating on a beating heart was almost unthinkable at this time. Day by day Helen tried to work out a way to save the "blue babies"—so called because of their bluish appearance caused by poorly oxygenated blood—born without pathways for good circulation from the heart to the lungs. Imagine gasping for air all the time.

Dressed in white gloves and a long white lab coat, Helen entered the fluoroscope room. The fluoroscope was an X-ray-type instrument that let her peek into the child's damaged heart. The machine was positioned behind the child to pass X-ray beams through the body. The fluoroscope light flickered and the beating heart's image was projected onto the screen. As the child turned, she was able to view the pulsating heart from all angles.

But Helen had a long way to go. With more and more children dying, she sought help from Canadian doctor Maude Abbott, who was considered the field's expert. Maude had collected many hearts, and as Helen examined them, patterns emerged. One conclusion was that these children were dying more from lack of oxygen than from their hearts giving out. Frustration mounted because although she could figure out the problem, she had no way to fix it.

There was one congenital defect that intrigued Helen more than others. The ductus arteriosus is a vessel connecting the pulmonary artery to the aorta while the baby is still a fetus. After birth this vessel usually collapses as the baby begins to breathe on its own. Sometimes this vessel remains open, which sends too much blood to the lungs, and in 1939, for the first time, pediatric surgeon Dr. Robert Gross operated to close off the vessel. Babies born without heart defects but with an open ductus needed the operation to close the ductus. But in the heart defect cases Helen studied, the baby with the open ductus did well because the baby received the oxygen it needed.

Could she design a surgery that would build or keep this vessel open in babies with a heart defect? To her it seemed a simple case of improved plumbing, bringing much-needed oxygen to the child.

Dr. Alfred Blalock had also operated successfully to close off the ductus. Helen watched one surgery at Johns Hopkins and said, "I stand in awe and admiration of your surgical skill, but the really great day will come when you build a ductus for a cyanotic child [blue baby]."

Brilliant surgical technician and researcher Mr. Vivien Thomas performed the first successful operation on a dog named Anna. Vivien knew that to replicate the defect of the "blue babies" he first had to reduce the amount of oxygen. He had to keep the dog alive for a few days and then restore the oxygen level with new plumbing to get the blood to the lungs. Anna's portrait still hangs in Johns Hopkins Medical School. In time Vivien practiced on more than 200 dogs. Was it time to try the risky surgery on one of the many sick babies? No one was sure.

On November 29, 1944, 18-month-old Eileen Saxon clung to life in her tiny oxygen tent. Without the surgery she'd die; with it she had a chance. Alfred Blalock wasn't sure he was ready to operate. He hadn't practiced enough. Helen convinced him it was Eileen's only chance.

Helen placed 8.8-pound Eileen on the operating table. Alfred had never performed this operation before, not even on an animal. Though not a doctor, Vivien was called to the operating room for support. Alfred and Helen needed him and his expertise. He stood directly behind Alfred. When Eileen survived the operation, her mother proclaimed, "When I saw Eileen for the first time, it was like a miracle. . . . I was beside myself with happiness." Unfortunately little Eileen died during a second operation several months later.

But by the third operation, the successes were clear. The patient was a six-year-old boy unable to walk because he wasn't getting enough oxygen. He entered the operating room with

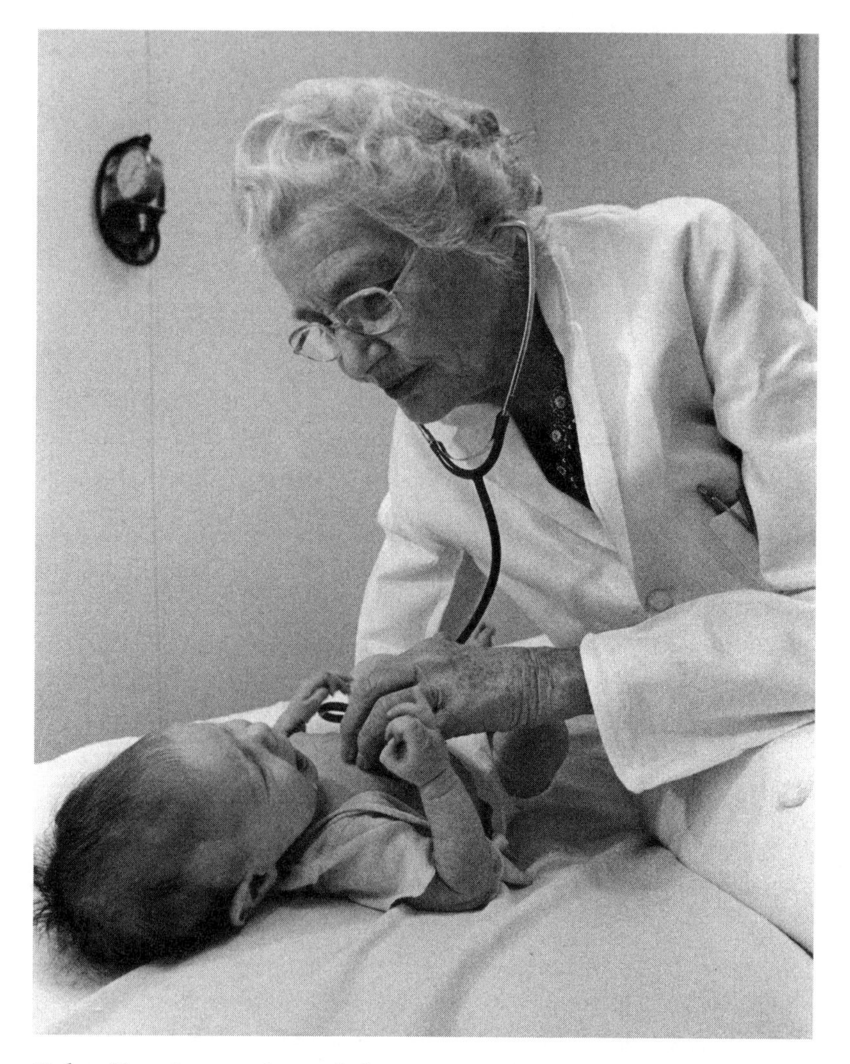

Helen Taussig examines a baby, 1980. *The Alan Chesney Medical Archives of the Johns Hopkins Medical Institutions*

deep blue skin and purple lips. After the final stitches were in place, the anesthesiologist said, "The boy's a lovely color now!"

Dr. Alfred Blalock's skilled hands, paired with Helen's and Vivien Thomas's research, led the way to a miracle: blue babies were turning pink. Although the surgery became known as the Blalock-Taussig shunt, it succeeded as much through Vivien's detailed research as through Alfred's and Helen's own skill. Vivien was African American, and many thought he didn't get adequate credit for that reason. The procedure eventually saved an estimated 12,000 children. Helen's medical students were so impressed with her compassion and knowledge of the human heart that they called themselves "the knights of Taussig."

Even with all she accomplished, the accolades would have been greater had she been a man. She said in the book *Particular Passions*, "Over the years I've gotten recognition for what I did, but I didn't at the time. It hurt for a while. It hurt when Dr. Blalock was elected to the National Academy of Arts and Sciences and I didn't even get promoted from an assistant professor to associate professor. Dr. Park always said, 'It's not your rank, it's what you do that counts' and he was right."

Helen was awarded the Medal of Freedom by Lyndon B. Johnson in 1964 with the citation stating, "Physician, physiologist and embryologist, her fundamental concepts have made possible the modern surgery of the heart which enables countless children to lead productive lives." She served as the American Heart Association's first female president.

Helen died in a car accident on May 20, 1986, a few days before her 88th birthday. Her legacy lives on in the founding of pediatric cardiology and the blue-baby operation, turning many blue babies a lovely shade of pink.

LEARN MORE

Breakthrough! How Three People Saved "Blue Babies" and Changed Medicine Forever by Jim Murphy (Clarion Books, 2015)

Leaders in Medicine by Shaun Hunter (Crabtree Publishing, 1999)

To Heal the Heart of a Child: Helen Taussig, M.D. by Joyce Baldwin (Walker, 1992)

Something the Lord Made (HBO Films, 2004)

Tiny Stitches: The Life of Medical Pioneer Vivien Thomas by Gwendolyn Hooks (Lee and Low, 2016)

Virginia Apgar

The Apgar Score

Nobody, but nobody, is going to stop breathing on me.

Medicine was not Virginia Apgar's first love. As a young girl at the beginning of the 20th century, she and her brother performed for their parents, Virginia on the violin or cello and Lawrence on the piano.

Fast-forward to the 1950s, when one of Virginia's patients, high school science teacher Carleen Hutchens, nervously awaited surgery. Carleen shared Virginia's love of music and had made her own violin, which she showed Virginia. The sound was beautiful, and Virginia thought she could find time in her busy schedule to make her own string instrument.

Carleen told Virginia she had found the perfect piece of wood for her violin. The only problem, Carleen said, was that it was currently in use as a phone booth shelf! Virginia was intrigued and asked the Columbia Presbyterian Medical Center if she could have the shelf out of the lobby phone booth. When they said no, she and Carleen devised plan B. Virginia fashioned a replacement shelf and stained it to match. Late one night with their tools hidden in a suitcase, Carleen went to work on removing the shelf with Virginia as the watchman.

Carleen came equipped with a handful of dimes, so if someone became suspicious she could pretend to make a phone call. Alas, the replacement shelf was too big. Off Carleen dashed to the nearest ladies' room to trim it to size and fit it back into the phone booth. That fine piece of former phone booth shelf became the curly maple back of Virginia's new handmade viola. Somehow, the *New York Times* found out and named it the great phone booth caper!

Virginia was born on June 7, 1909, to Helen and Charles Apgar in Westfield, New Jersey. As a young girl, Virginia sat by her father's side as he looked through his homemade telescope. When it was her turn, she peered into the lens at the stars lighting up the sky. She shared his love of science and invention. With her mother often busy taking care of her ill brother, Lawrence, Virginia spent many hours in her father's basement laboratory, where he conducted scientific experiments on radio waves.

By the time Virginia entered high school, she knew two things: One, she wanted to go to college; and two, she wanted to study medicine. At Mount Holyoke College in South Hadley, Massachusetts, Virginia studied zoology to learn about animals. Armed with a bachelor of arts degree in zoology and a minor in chemistry, Virginia began medical school at Columbia University's College of Physicians and Surgeons. She graduated in 1933, fourth in her class.

She began her residency in the competitive field of surgery. Dr. Alan Whipple, the chair of surgery, admired her grit and intelligence. Then he did something that would be considered

Virginia Apgar admiring her instrument, made from a phone booth shelf, 1966. *Library of Congress*

highly unethical today, although he thought it was in her best interest. He told her to switch specialties to one that held more opportunities for women. At first she was concerned; she liked surgery and had completed two years already. Why should she change now and have to begin again?

The women Alan Whipple knew in surgery had trouble getting enough patients for a successful practice. He suggested Virginia investigate anesthesiology, which was a new field of medicine. Up until this time, nurse-anesthetists handled putting patients to sleep during surgery. But improvements in anesthesiology were leading to improvements in surgery. Virginia could be in at the very beginning.

When she had trouble finding a paying anesthesiologist residency training, Virginia stayed on to finish her surgical training. She had amassed large loans for college and medical school and decided to worry about anesthesiology training after she became debt free.

She pieced together her training, learning from nurse-anesthetists and Dr. Ralph Waters's anesthesia department in Madison, Wisconsin. Next she moved back to New York City to Bellevue Hospital for more training. Housing was her greatest concern. She couldn't live with the male residents, and no one had thought to set up housing for the women. She ended up bunking in the maids' quarters of the Bellevue Clinic building!

In 1939 Virginia became the second woman to be board certified in the new field of anesthesiology. Shortly after, at only 30 years old, she was appointed head of the new division at Columbia Presbyterian Hospital. Virginia set up the new division by creating an organizational chart complete with the number of residents to be added each year.

As an anesthesiologist Virginia always visited her anxious patients the day before surgery. She had a calming manner. One young child feared elevators, so on the day of surgery she carried him down the stairs to surgery. She was always the first one to help and carried a pocketknife and breathing tube in her purse just in case someone needed an emergency tracheotomy (a hole cut through the neck into the windpipe, allowing a patient to breathe).

As a new specialty, anesthesiology functioned under the department of surgery. In 1949, after 11 years at the top, Virginia was pushed aside for a man as the division became its own department. Because she had been passed over, she suddenly had much more time to devote to her tiniest patients.

She was appointed full professor of anesthesiology, the first full professor ever in the new field. By this time Virginia had delivered many babies and noticed how little was recorded with each birth. She set out to standardize the examinations done at birth, painstakingly noting how many babies still died even in the hospital. It is unbelievable by today's standards, but no one examined the newborns to catch critical health issues that should be corrected immediately. Instead nurses whisked the babies away to be weighed, measured, and wrapped in a blanket.

She focused on ways to grade the babies by making a list of health measurements. After studying the data from 1949 to 1952, she pared the list to five signs. These signs, now known as the Apgar score, were read in the first minute of the baby's life and then again within the first five minutes. This way doctors were able to decide how much, if any, extra care the baby needed.

Ten years after she identified the five signs, known first as the Newborn Scoring System, Dr. Joseph Butterfield, a Colorado pediatrician, came up with an easy acronym to remember the signs using Virginia's last name. Often those new to the method didn't realize the score was named after a real person. Virginia once told Joseph Butterfield that she was greeted by a Boston Hospital secretary who said, "Oh, I didn't know Apgar was a person; I thought it was just a thing!"

The doctors looked at *A* for appearance or color of the baby, *P* for pulse or heart rate, *G* for grimace or irritability when its reflexes were stimulated, *A* for activity or muscle tone, and *R* for respiration.

	0	1	2
Heart rate	Absent	<100 per minute	100–140 per minute
Respiration	Absent	Irregular	Strong, crying
Reflex irritability	Absent	Weak	Grimace, sneeze
Muscle tone	Flaccid	Some flexion	Stong flexion
Color	Blue	Extremities blue	Pink

Two possible points were scored for each sign, with a perfect score equaling 10. When a newborn scored mostly twos, it was considered healthy; mostly ones and it was in need of some assistance, such as oxygen to help breathing; and a baby scoring mostly zeroes was in immediate danger.

The Apgar score provided a standard way to evaluate all newborn babies. It is still used all over the world and gives babies a great start in life.

Virginia encountered many birth defects while attending more than 17,000 births. With her system she was able to correlate the defects with the kind of Apgar score the baby had received at birth. Her successful career was dependent on her need for ongoing learning, and in 1959 she enrolled at Johns Hopkins University to earn a master's degree in public health.

She decided not to go back to work as an anesthesiologist and instead joined the National Foundation for Infantile Paralysis (NFIP). The NFIP was begun as an organization to help polio victims. In fact it was the same organization that Sister

NEONATOLOGY

Neonatology is the specialty of medicine dealing with newborns, sick babies, or premature babies. If a newborn needs extra care, it may be admitted to the Neonatal Intensive Care Unit, known as the NICU. Some babies are full term, while others are born before 37 weeks' gestation and are known as premature babies. Premature babies need extra oxygen and/or a respirator to help them breathe because their lungs haven't fully developed. They may spend time in an incubator where they can be kept warm. Babies in the NICU sometimes have digestive problems and require tiny IVs to be inserted to make sure they get good nutrition.

The NICU is a separate area from where healthy newborns are kept, and the NICU doctors and nurses are specifically trained to help these very sick babies. Neonatologists must attend four years of college and medical school followed by a three-year pediatric residency and a three-year neonatology fellowship for additional training.

Elizabeth Kenny had first fought but ultimately became united with in her treatment for polio.

With the success of the polio vaccine in the 1950s and 1960s, the NFIP changed its direction. The organization became the National Foundation–March of Dimes and focused on birth defects.

Virginia was named the Division of Congenital Malformations director for the March of Dimes. She was responsible for research programs, fund-raising, and educating the public on various birth defects. Many years ago babies with birth defects were shunned, and doctors told parents that their child should be placed in an institution. Virginia knew many of these children could be helped, and she traveled around the country educating the public on avoiding birth defects in the first place, as well as helping those children already stricken. In time she rose to the position of senior vice president for the March of Dimes.

According to Dr. L. Stanley James, Virginia "lifted birth defects from a secret closet and put them firmly on the map. Through her vigor and drive their [March of Dimes] income increased from $19 million when she first arrived to $46 million when she died." She also encouraged the March of Dimes to look for ways to prevent birth defects by preventing preterm births. She coined the slogan, "Be good to your baby before it's born."

She was once asked if women in medicine were discriminated against. She said, "Heavens, no. Never! You just had to be twice as smart as the men."

Virginia did everything fast, and once when speaking at an international meeting, she found out many in the audience had not understood a word. But they arrived at the essence because "it was not what she said, but how she said it." She also drove fast and loved the wind in her hair, claiming that her "tires never wore out because they never touched the ground."

Virginia died in her sleep on August 7, 1974, at the age of 65. At her funeral close friend Dr. L. Stanley James said, "With her, life was exciting; her youthful enthusiasm and energy were boundless. She was warm and compassionate, and at the same time had a great sense of humor, sometimes earthy. Integrity was her hallmark: she was utterly sincere and honest and could not tolerate any form of deception. . . . All these qualities together with her magnetism and charm, contributed to her greatness."

In 2001 the *New England Journal of Medicine* said the Apgar score is still the best predictor of infant health in the first month.

LEARN MORE

Headstrong: 52 Women Who Changed Science and the World by Rachel Swaby (Broadway Books, 2015)

Virginia Apgar: Innovative Female Physician and Inventor of the Apgar Score by Melanie Ann Apel (Rosen Central, 2004)

Women and Medicine by Beatrice Levin (Scarecrow Press, 2002)

PART III

And Today Still Fighting

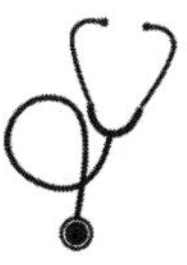

True, women's hearts tend to be smaller, and perhaps the tissues are a bit more delicate, but a woman's heart is no less mighty than a man's. They are equally persistent.

—KATHY MAGLIATO

On April 25, 2015, a 7.8-magnitude earthquake struck Nepal and triggered an avalanche, nearly wiping out Mt. Everest Base Camp. Dr. Rachel Tullet, a British specialist in emergency medicine, was working at the emergency tent on the base camp and said in a May 2015 article in *Guardian*, "I saw it coming. I knew instantly it was going to get us, to reach our camp." The force of the avalanche threw Rachel into a rock and buried her in snow and ice. Even with a cracked patella (kneecap), an open wound, and torn ligaments, Rachel jumped into action.

Rachel struggled to walk and improvised by using a climbing pole as a crutch. She helped save many lives. Along with Dr. Megan Walmsley, an Australian anesthetist, she calmly organized triage and treated over 80 people, including 25 critically injured patients. Selina Dicker, a climber from London, said in an article from the *Guardian*, "She [Rachel] was an absolute superwoman. I've no doubt that far more people would have died if she hadn't been there."

The women practicing medicine from the late 20th century to today are the modern pioneers of medicine. Most, like Rachel, are not the first in their respective fields. However, like those before them, these women have an ability to assess the situations they find themselves in and figure out the best course of action.

The women's movement of the 1960s and '70s ultimately helped women such as Rachel succeed. In 1961 women made up 5.8 percent of total medical school enrollment. Ten years later that figure had climbed to nearly 11 percent. Women are now admitted to medical school at nearly an equal rate as men. In 2015–2016 women made up 47 percent of medical school enrollees.

Various careers in medicine became popular for women during the 1970s. Beyond nurses and doctors, physician assistants and occupational and physical therapists added women to their ranks. According to the Bureau of Labor Statistics, nearly 80 percent of workers in the health-care and social assistance field are women, outnumbering men four to one.

Even today there are ongoing challenges for women in medicine, especially in terms of wages. In a study published in the *Journal of the American Medical Association (JAMA) Internal Medicine* (July 2016), salaries were analyzed for over 10,000 academic physicians at 24 US medical schools. The study, adjusted for age, experience, and faculty rank, showed that the average pay gap between men and women was $19,878 a year. Without this adjustment the pay gap was over $51,000 a year. The study also found that women physicians were less likely to be full professors. The Medscape Physician Compensation Report of 2016 states that overall, women physicians make 24 percent less than their male peers.

Just like their predecessors, contemporary medical women battle disease, injury, and illness and help those who cannot help themselves. Catherine Hamlin thought she would be staying in Ethiopia for three years, setting up a midwifery school. But when she discovered the great need of the fistula patients, she never left. Adele Levine works every day to improve the lives of war amputees as well as civilians who need physical therapy. She helps to heal these stricken heroes, restoring their mobility and confidence. Dr. Kathy Magliato fought hard for her place in the male-dominated field of cardiothoracic surgery. Her steady hands and calm demeanor give her patients a new beginning. Dr. Bonnie Mason gracefully reinvented herself when all looked lost by mentoring young doctors through their tough odds. Jerri Nielsen faced her own mortality as she battled breast cancer on the ice-covered continent of Antarctica.

Edna Adan Ismail teaches girls undergoing unspeakable abuse in Somaliland that education is the way to achieve dreams. Dr. Sister Anne Brooks gives both tough love and compassion to the poor in Mississippi; and Dr. Sherrie Ballantine-Talmadge shows young athletes with concussions and injuries the road back to health and school. Each of these medical women has tackled serious problems, leading the way and encouraging more women to study medicine and work in the health-care field.

Catherine Hamlin

The Fistula Pilgrims

We're giving a young, beautiful woman a new life, and this is why I stay in Ethiopia. I love them.

Catherine Hamlin's Australian upbringing had taught her it was wonderful to help. She and her husband, Reginald, both gynecologists, believed they had much to offer those who were less privileged, and living in their comfortable suburban house in Adelaide, Australia, in 1959, they felt unfulfilled.

Scouring the medical journals for jobs, they spotted an ad looking for doctors to work at the Princess Tsehai Memorial Hospital and open a midwifery school in Addis Ababa, Ethiopia. They signed a three-year contract, noting that they could always leave when the time was up. They packed up and, along with their six-year-old son, Richard, moved to Ethiopia.

The fresh scent of eucalyptus mixed with dust in every breath instantly reminded them of Australia. Just off the plane,

Catherine Hamlin at the Addis Ababa Fistula Hospital, Ethiopia, 2009. *Wikimedia Commons*

their first task was to find the town and the hospital. Someone was supposed to have met them. When no one arrived, they set off on foot, unknowingly in the wrong direction. They walked along the fragmented road carrying their luggage and seeing nothing but green countryside (for it was just after the spring rains), loaded-down donkeys, and a few cars. With no town or hospital in sight, they turned around and began again.

"Reg said, 'Don't worry, Cath', I'll take you home next Saturday.' She responded, 'We can't go home. We've only just arrived.'"

Catherine Nicholson was born on January 24, 1924, in Sydney, Australia. As a child Catherine loved to climb trees and ride horses and was once caught throwing mud pies at her governess. With this great spirit, she knew early on that she wanted to help others and at some point decided to become a physician. She graduated from the University of Sydney Medical School in 1946.

When she and Reg arrived in Ethiopia in 1959, the sights and smells immediately piqued Catherine's curiosity. They spent their very first night in the dark because the previous gynecologist hadn't paid his electric bills. Candles, bread, and sardines rounded out the evening.

The next day they began a new journey going about the business of opening the new midwifery school. The hospital had opened in 1951, and the midwifery school was part of Emperor Haile Selassie's plan.

Immediately the doctors discovered the roughness of Ethiopia. There weren't many good roads, there were few hospitals, and women in the midst of childbirth were without trained care.

Young girls in Ethiopia and other poor African countries are forced to marry young and become pregnant as early as 13 or 14. Their narrow pelvises make delivery difficult, often causing obstructed labor and stillborn babies. A prolonged labor injures internal organs, resulting in an obstetric fistula, which is a hole between organs in the birth canal. The victims are left without control over their bladders, bowels, or both.

Fistulas used to be common worldwide. Improved medical care in America eradicated obstetric fistulas in 1895. When delivery goes wrong in a modern country, the medical professionals step in to use forceps or perform a cesarean section.

The fistula patients are shunned throughout Africa and undeveloped countries all over the world because they can't keep themselves clean. Husbands divorce them, and they are sent to live in remote huts, sometimes dying. When asked about their horrible situations, many say the loneliness is the worst.

Initially Catherine and Reg Hamlin stayed on call 24 hours a day. They struggled to communicate with their patients because the Ethiopian language is completely different from European languages. The Hamlins picked up necessary phrases, and local medical staff interpreted.

The fistula patients broke Catherine's heart from the start. She had come to Ethiopia to train midwives and perform routine gynecology; what she found in the fistula patients instead were women in dire need of relief. One of Catherine's first patients was a 17-year-old who had given birth in a rural area. The baby was stillborn after the mother had been in labor for five days. With her bladder destroyed, urine rained down her legs. Catherine didn't know how to help, so she sent the girl to a German gynecologist at a nearby hospital. The Hamlins educated themselves on treatments and surgeries for the women.

Another of Catherine's early fistula patients arrived after walking almost 280 miles. Dressed in nothing but rags, she reeked of urine. Ten years earlier she had suffered two holes in her bladder. After her operation Catherine presented her with a new dress in which to go home. The patient waved good-bye at the bus station with bright eyes and said, "God will reward you for all you have done for me."

The women—Reg named them fistula pilgrims—had suffered more than any woman ever should. Catherine and Reg wondered if they could build a hospital dedicated to fistula treatment, as well as space for the women to live while waiting for their surgeries.

Government unrest stalled their plans. In 1960 the head of the emperor's bodyguard service staged a revolt while the emperor was out of the country. Gunfire broke out just as Catherine was delivering a baby. Later at home bullets flew, and she found herself in the middle of the volley. She ducked low in the hall while gunfire hit the house, flying through a window and penetrating a wall in the dining room where they had just finished a meal.

As soon as a lull occurred, she, Reg, and their son, Richard, made their way to the thick-walled hospital. They slept on mattresses on the floor, and the couple treated the many casualties.

FISTULA TREATMENT

Fistula repair through surgery was not considered possible until the early 19th century. Before that time patients were treated with catheters (tubes to drain the bladder) and primitive tampons to manage leakage. In the 1850s a treatment procedure was outlined by Dr. James Sims of Lancaster, North Carolina. James discovered how best to view the fistula by using a bent spoon, which eventually became the modern-day speculum (a device used to dilate the vagina and cervix).

Despite his advances, James still didn't know how to close a fistula. He worked tirelessly, sometimes operating on the same patient many times. His methods were not always ethical, and many of his early supporters abandoned him. His patients suffered excruciating pain from his obsession with finding a cure. He at last achieved success with Anarcha, an enslaved 17-year-old girl, when he used fine silver wires to close up the fistula. He had operated on her 30 times, without anesthetic! Dr. James Sims used this method repeatedly on all of his patients, including those he had given up hope of ever curing. He built the first hospital for the sole reason of fistula treatment and is known as the father of modern gynecology.

The Ethiopian army restored peace, and the emperor returned to power. After the attempted coup, Reg kept a revolver, but the best protection they possessed, according to Catherine, was Rangi, Richard's pet bull terrier, and later a second bull terrier, Juno.

Catherine could not quit on the fistula pilgrims. As they left on a desperately needed holiday to Australia, the Hamlins were asked if they would be coming back. Catherine said,

> There was never any question about not coming back. It was wonderful to visit friends and family and to enjoy luxuries like ice creams and milkshakes, but while we were on holiday our thoughts often turned to Ethiopia and the fistula pilgrims whom we knew would be waiting our return. We felt we had at least ten years work ahead of us before the Ethiopians would be able to take over their care. Although we still had strong ties to Australia and New Zealand, now we also had a stake in Ethiopia.

Catherine filled her days with surgeries and deliveries. After one particularly difficult day, she stretched out to rest and wondered how her patient in labor was progressing. She walked back to the hospital to check the baby. "I listened and had a feeling of dread. I could not hear the heartbeat at all. It was obvious that the patient was in strong labour, so I quickly gave her oxygen and an ether anesthetic to stop the contractions. As she stopped pushing the heartbeat slowly came back. . . . After a lot of anxiety we delivered a beautiful, live baby. If I had arrived a few minutes later, the baby would have died. I felt quite certain I was guided to go at that time."

With new fistula patients arriving daily, a hospital dedicated to the women was certainly the answer. The government wouldn't provide financing, so on their next visit home to Australia, the Hamlins tried to raise the funds.

After her return to Ethiopia, Catherine headed out for a ride on her horse. She spotted a beautiful piece of land near the river. On the same day that Catherine found the land and it was deemed available, a large donation arrived from America. Catherine believed she saw "God's clear guidance" over this purchase. The Hamlins fought for permits, permissions, and supplies in addition to money.

In 1974, while still early in the hospital's construction, a group called the Armed Forces Coordinating Committee, known as the Dergue, staged a coup, ousting the emperor. Ethiopia had been hit by a serious famine, and the people revolted against the emperor with corruption charges. Again, bullets flew. Catherine was knitting on the couch when she rose to answer the phone. Her friend Pippa Sandford called to ask if she was reporting to the British embassy for safety as had been suggested.

Catherine replied that she didn't feel she could leave the fistula pilgrims. Suddenly a bullet soared into the house, piercing the sofa cushion where she had been sitting. She jumped and said, "Oh, Pippa, you may have just saved my life."

During the unrest construction on the hospital continued. Catherine believed the new Communist government didn't interfere because the Hamlins treated the patients for free. Nevertheless, Catherine didn't want to draw attention by hosting a grand opening for the new hospital. On May 24, 1975, Catherine said, "Reg and I, alone, cut a ribbon strung between two chairs in the drawing room of our house and declared the Addis Ababa Fistula Hospital open. Next day we began treating our first patients."

In 1991 Reg was diagnosed with cancer. The tumor was removed, and at first all was well, but the lump began to grow

DESTA MENDER

There are some fistula patients who cannot be healed and some who need extra recovery time. For these women Catherine built Desta Mender on the edge of Addis Ababa in 2001. Desta Mender, meaning joy village, consists of plain white houses with tin roofs and can house about 50 women. They learn skills they can use when they return to their communities, such as spinning silk, vegetable gardening, and working in the orchards and dairies. Desta Mender gives the women both financial and emotional support so they can become valuable members of the community.

back after three months. The doctors tried radiation to no avail. When her beloved Reg died of cancer on August 5, 1993, Catherine wondered if she would be able to carry on without him. "On this occasion I was suddenly overwhelmed with the feeling that everything was too much for me and that I would never be able to run the hospital by myself," she wrote. "I was not crying but evidently looked as though I was, as Birru [a trusted aid and a man with a soft heart] appeared and knelt by my chair. He took my hand in his, kissed the back of it and said, 'Don't leave us; we'll all help you.'"

Birru's words encouraged Catherine, and she counted her blessings. The future was cheerful and positive. At present the hospital does more fistula repairs than any other hospital in the world. They have treated more than 43,000 women, 95 percent of them successfully.

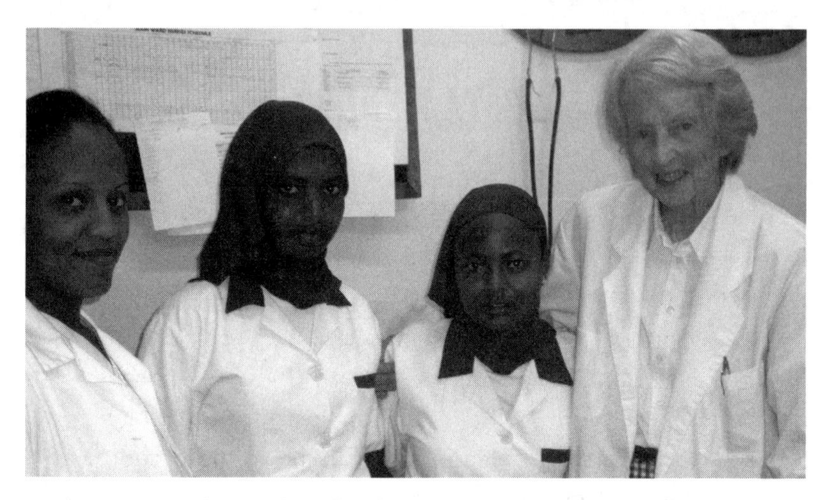

Catherine Hamlin with midwifery students at the Hamlin College of Midwives, 2009. *Wikimedia Commons*

Twice nominated for the Nobel Peace Prize, Catherine believed more than ever in preventing the fistula injuries. To that end the Hamlin College of Midwives was finally founded in 2006.

At the age of 93, as of this writing, Dr. Catherine Hamlin still oversees the hospital, continually training people to carry on her work. At her 90th birthday party in 2013, Catherine said, "We have to eradicate Ethiopia of this awful thing that's happening to women: suffering, untold suffering, in the countryside. I leave this with you to do in the future, to carry on."

LEARN MORE

Addis Ababa Fistula Hospital and the Hamlin College of Midwives, https://hamlin.org.au

The Hospital by the River: A Story of Hope by Catherine Hamlin (Monarch Books, 2004)

Edna Adan Ismail

The Dump That Became a Hospital

Don't ever underestimate the capacity of a human being who is determined to do something.

Edna followed her father around the remote hospital. A doctor, he gave the girl instructions such as *hold the patient's hand, roll up this bandage*, or *run an errand*. Edna did the best she could because she wanted to help. But she did not always have the skills, and often the hospital didn't have the right equipment or supplies. It was then that Edna decided she would build a hospital, one that her father would appreciate.

Edna Adan was born on September 8, 1937, in the city of Hargeisa, Somaliland. Because her father was a doctor and her mother the daughter of the postmaster general, she had a privileged upbringing.

While Edna's family was elite and educated, Edna's mother still believed in the Somali custom of female circumcision,

Edna Adan Ismail looking over the city of Hargeisa. *Sarah Winfield, courtesy of Edna Adan Ismail*

or female genital mutilation (FGM). Young girls between the age of five and nine undergo this procedure in which healthy genital tissue is cut and the remaining area stitched up. The scar tissue that forms is unable to stretch, resulting in a birth canal not big enough for safe labor and delivery. Historically FGM has been performed to reduce promiscuity and to make sure girls were eligible for marriage. The misconception is that it must be done for religious reasons, even though Islam forbids it.

Edna's mother waited until her father was away for the procedure to be performed. "I was not consulted, I was caught, held down, and it was done. My mother thought it was the right thing to do." Her father disagreed vehemently, and her parents' relationship suffered. His fierce reaction influenced Edna against the practice.

Education was important to Edna's parents, and even though it wasn't common, their daughter was educated as well as their sons. Learning side by side with the boys was not permitted, however, so Edna listened from the next room while her brothers were tutored, learning by immersion. At 15 she was sent to a new nearby elementary school for girls to student teach for part of the day, and in the afternoon to be taught by the teacher who instructed the boys.

SOMALILAND

The breakaway Republic of Somaliland is situated on the Horn of Africa. When Edna Adan was born, Somaliland was a territory of the United Kingdom. In 1960 Somaliland achieved its independence and promptly united with the former Italian colony of Somalia. Civil war broke out in the late 1980s, and the country was devastated by violence. More than 500,000 Somalis died, with a similar number of refugees fleeing to Ethiopia. In 1991 the Republic of Somaliland achieved a new independence and the recovery began in this democratic, yet still unrecognized country on the Horn of Africa.

Because she was smart, Edna was allowed to take a scholarship exam normally reserved for boys. The results came in and Edna qualified, becoming the first Somali girl to study nursing in Great Britain. After seven years of study, she became Somalia's first midwife.

Her father taught her many things, including the washing of forceps and how to make bandages out of old bed sheets. But what he really taught her, according to Edna, "was compassion and the value of looking after the sick. One of his favorite expressions was 'if you cannot do it with your heart, your hands will never do it.'"

Originally, Edna's passion was surgery. But as a young nurse in London, her father said that surgery was fine, "but what are you going to do for women when they are having a baby?"

Today Edna is grateful that her father planted this seed in her brain. She said, "You're with women at a time when she's most afraid and a time when she's most vulnerable. She places herself in your hands and the life of her baby in your hands and you have to do the best you can for both mother and baby and the family." Without her father's advice, she would've missed the human relationship with women that midwifery brings to health care.

First in many things, Edna also became the first woman to drive in her country and then became the true "first lady" by marrying Somaliland's prime minister, Ibrahim Egal.

When Edna's marriage failed, she joined the World Health Organization (WHO), working as a nursing expert, advisor, and regional technical officer for maternal/child health. Edna traveled the world with the WHO and the United Nations while civil war devastated her homeland. Her poor countrywomen back home suffered through needless diseases and poor maternal care. But what could she do to help them? She was determined to do what she could.

Building a private hospital might help! She had a place in Mogadishu, Somalia's capital, picked out, but fierce fighting and dangerous conditions during the civil war forced her to abandon her effort.

Edna could have retired peacefully in London or Paris, but the desperate needs of women in Somaliland beckoned her. Then the newly formed breakaway Republic of Somaliland offered Edna land to build her hospital, but the land was far from the center of town. She argued that the distant land would be too remote for women to reach in the middle of the night because babies didn't wait. Next the government offered her a small strip of land that had been used as an execution ground during the civil war and later as a garbage dump.

Edna was disappointed. The former dump was in a very poor part of town, but Edna realized this was the area where her patients lived and needed the hospital most. Could Edna transform the dump into a hospital?

She cashed in her WHO pension and sold all of her belongings, including her Mercedes. She spent $300,000 of her own money to build the hospital. She says she misses her car, but "what it has become gives me far more satisfaction. The forceps, the instruments, the construction material that it has helped to provide is far more exciting. . . . Besides, what would I do with a Mercedes in a country that has no paved roads?"

The white, three-story building was nearly complete. When it came time for the roof, Edna had run out of money. The *New York Times* ran an article presenting Edna's dilemma, and her money problems improved with the help of worldwide donors. She also bargained for cement and other building materials from local businesses. Edna's hospital opened in 2002 and is capable of housing 69 patients.

What was once a place of terror, misery, and hardship has become a place of happy births and joy. The dump "was a sore, an ulcer in the center of town. The government carted away 32 truckloads of garbage from it. Now I live in it. I wouldn't be anywhere else in the world. That's my home, my hospital, that's where I hope to spend whatever days God gives me."

One result of the violent civil war was that Somaliland's health-care system was completely ruined, with mothers and infants suffering the brunt of the collapse. Currently Somalia has one of highest maternal mortality rates in the world. Statistics from the WHO in 2015 indicate that in Somalia there are 732 maternal deaths for every 100,000 live births. Somaliland statistics are unavailable since the country is unrecognized.

Edna's statistics tell a different story. For the patients she cares for, the maternal mortality rate is now 312 deaths per 100,000 births. She is making a difference.

In Somaliland Edna has sought to change what women have and what they can do. One of the most dangerous things a woman can do there is become pregnant. The odds are high that they could die. If you're a woman or girl in Somaliland, you have to receive permission from your husband, father, or brother for medical care. Imagine not being able to see a doctor or nurse if you're sick or need an operation simply because your father or brother or husband doesn't approve.

Improving health care in these countries is not just about making it more available, it is also about teaching the women what kind of treatment they need. The education that Edna strives for teaches women the importance of prenatal checkups, immunizations, and breast-feeding. Edna addressed a TEDx conference in 2011, where she spoke on the importance of education: "Education is one of the strongest gifts we can give a human being and particularly a woman in Africa."

Doubting officials surrounded Edna, and many thought she had aspired to an impossible dream. But Edna was not to be stopped. Building the hospital was only the beginning for Edna. Before the hospital was completed, she had trained 30 nurses. The nursing candidates completed a three-year general nurse training, as well as midwifery and laboratory technician training.

Edna knows what it is like to keep fighting and offers advice to women everywhere. "Don't just take it lying down and say, 'Oh, but I am a woman, I need to accept what comes to me.' Don't be fatalistic about your future, your career. Aim for it. Go for it. Fight for it. Campaign for it. Study for it. Compete for it and get it. Otherwise, it's not going to happen."

One of Edna's main objectives in opening her hospital was to provide midwife training. She said at the 2011 WHO conference briefing of the state of the world's midwifery, "The world needs midwives who are time-effective, cost-effective and capable of saving lives."

Edna's goal of training 1,000 midwives is aggressive, but she hasn't backed down. She founded the Edna Adan University in 2009 and just graduated the third class of midwives in 2015. Each of the 40 new community midwives was awarded a midwifery kit complete with delivery instruments, resuscitation equipment, sponges, scales, stethoscopes, and headlights. They can now go out into the community to help deliver babies safely.

Another mission of the Edna Adan Maternity Hospital is to stop FGM. The WHO estimates that approximately 140 million women have endured FGM, and every year three million more girls are at risk. Awareness and education of the health risks are the keys to eliminate this practice, and Edna continues to fight diligently.

Edna Adan Ismail with community midwife graduates in Hargeisa, Somaliland, 2015. *Sarah Winfield, courtesy of Edna Adan Ismail*

Edna says, "FGM has no place as far as religion is concerned because Islam forbids it; it has no place in medicine because it is harmful and damaging; it has no place to prevent promiscuity or preserve virginity, because it is the upbringing of that girl that protects her morals and her virginity. So female genital mutilation has no place in this day and age."

At nearly 80 years old, Edna has amazing drive. "This little hospital—built on a garbage dump by a crazy old woman who should have retired a long time ago—has reduced maternal mortality rate of the women who come here to one-quarter of the national average," she says. "And if Somaliland can do it—a poor country that is not politically recognized, then any other country can do it, too."

LEARN MORE

"Edna Adan Ismail—If We Can Train Midwives in Somaliland, Everyone Can!" TEDx Conference, Geneva, 2011, www.youtube.com/watch?v=hxJ8LELZCjo

Edna Adan Maternity Hospital, www.ednahospital.org

Ethiopia, Djibouti and Somaliland by Jean-Bernard Carillet (Lonely Planet Publications, 2013)

Half the Sky: Turning Oppression into Opportunity for Women Worldwide by Nicholas Kristof and Sheryl WuDunn (Vintage Books, 2010)

Anne Brooks

Sister Doctor with Attitude

I have come to believe that the key in the ignition is hope, and that my job is to empower people to have the courage to put that key into the ignition of their lives.

As a young girl, Anne Brooks became quite good at walking on eggshells so as not to disturb her alcoholic mother. Her navy captain father was away fighting in World War II, and Anne took care of her mother day in and day out.

When the war ended and her father returned, she recalls sitting upstairs listening to her parents fight and crying "because I didn't want my parents killing each other."

Anne Brooks was born in Washington, DC, in 1938. Her parents divorced in 1948 when she was 10, and her already unstable life changed again. Anne begged her father to take her with him to Key West, Florida. But she couldn't stay in the officers'

Dr. Sister Anne Brooks at the Tutwiler Clinic, Tutwiler, Mississippi. *Courtesy of Sister Anne Brooks*

quarters where he was assigned. Instead her father deposited her at a convent boarding school. She wasn't Catholic and didn't even attend church.

The nuns, dressed in their long, flowing habits, whooshed around Anne. She was terrified with this unfamiliar life and continued to feel unloved. One day while playing, she spotted Sister Henri Ferdinand scouring a toilet on her hands and knees. A shocked Anne told Sister Henri, "This work is not for you. This is dirty work."

Sister Henri told Anne that there was no dirty work when you worked for God, and this work was part of taking care of Anne and the other students. Anne had never heard such a thing. But this lesson stuck with her, and from that time on, Anne felt loved. Because of their ease and selflessness, Anne began to trust the nuns and wanted to emulate them. They were now her family.

The nuns gave her a safe haven in the midst of her troubled family and a model for her own life. She converted to Catholicism when she was a freshman in high school and made her first vows in the religious order of the Sisters of the Holy Names of Jesus and Mary when she was 17, in 1955.

For many physicians an illness of their own or of a loved one is what pushed them toward the medical community. This was the case for Anne. During her religious training, her knees began to ache. Someone suggested it was the intense kneeling; however, other parts of her young body ached, too. The doctors diagnosed her with rheumatoid arthritis. The constant pain forced her to rest in bed at least half of every day. Nevertheless, Anne enrolled at Barry University in Miami, Florida, where she earned a degree in elementary education. She began teaching in a Florida Catholic school, where she rolled down the long hallways in a wheelchair. Controlling the pain was becoming more difficult even as she swallowed the 40 aspirin each day, as ordered by her doctor.

Sister Anne's own body was attacking her joints, and in a desperate move, she was admitted to a rehabilitation hospital in Boston for six months. There she received injections to help control her immune system. Sister Anne was well enough to return to teaching on crutches. She taught in Florida for about 17 years, eventually serving as principal. In 1972 she was assigned to a new, very affluent school.

Sister Anne had always felt her abilities lay in teaching those who really needed her, impoverished students who didn't have other opportunities. She felt out of place with the well-to-do children, so she supplemented her teaching with volunteer work at a free clinic run by Dr. John Upledger, an osteopathic physician. To Sister Anne's surprise, John told her he could relieve her pain. She didn't believe him until he began to treat her with acupuncture, osteopathic manipulation (which strives to improve joint range of motion), and nutrition. She was able to throw away the back brace she'd been told to wear.

A few years later, John moved to Michigan to join the faculty at Michigan State University College of Osteopathic Medicine.

He and Sister Anne kept in touch. In 1978 John convinced Sister Anne that she could help many more people as a physician. At first she thought he was crazy; she'd barely passed chemistry

OSTEOPATHIC MEDICINE

The American Association of Colleges of Osteopathic Medicine (AACOM) regulates 33 accredited osteopathic medical colleges in the United States. Osteopathic medical students represent more than 20 percent (approximately 26,100 future physicians) of all medical students in the United States for the academic year 2015–2016. Currently osteopathic doctors represent 8 percent of all practicing US physicians.

Andrew Thomas Still founded osteopathic medicine in June 1874 in Kirksville, Missouri. He had been a traditional medical doctor who had become dissatisfied with the medical practices of the day because he felt they did more harm than good. He developed a medical care system that promoted the body's innate ability to heal itself, naming it *osteon*, meaning bone, and *pathos*, meaning to suffer. Osteopathic doctors (DOs) practice in all specialties.

Osteopathic doctors believe that the structure of the body impacts its function, so if the structure is injured in some way, it can cause problems in the rest of the body. Once the proper structure is restored through manipulative treatments, the path is cleared for the body to heal itself.

in high school. But after securing a scholarship to osteopathic medical school, she was on her way at the age of 40.

After Anne completed her training, she set out to find a place to work. The National Public Health Corps scholarship she had accepted stipulated that she give back and find an underprivileged community in which to practice. Anne sent out many query letters to cities across the south. Only one city responded: Tutwiler, Mississippi, the town where W. C. Handy discovered the blues in 1905. When she arrived in 1983, the small, impoverished town was singing the blues.

The town's previous doctor had skipped out of the poor Mississippi delta town and left the small clinic shuttered. Anne had to convince the town she was serious and planned to reopen the one-story brick clinic. She said, "I was looking for the bottom of the barrel, and Tutwiler is it."

Anne took charge in 1983, and the first thing she did was to take down the wall in the waiting room that originally divided white and black patients. The rooms were no longer segregated but had not been remodeled. As she began her practice, she learned to approach her patients from the side. She never looked at them head-on, eye to eye. They didn't trust her, and many of the African American patients believed that if you looked a white woman in the eyes, you might get in trouble.

The people who live in Tutwiler are some of the poorest in the United States. Some can pay for their care, some can't. But they are proud people, says Anne, and they often pay with work such as cleaning the clinic's gutters or other odd jobs. Some pay a bit in dollars and the rest in squash or tomatoes. Donations make up most of the clinic's day-to-day expenses.

One patient had a way with quilts and made one for Anne to pay for her hospital care. The staff at the Tutwiler Clinic encouraged her, and other women joined the quilting circle in 1988.

Today they are known as the Tutwiler Quilters and sell their unique quilts online, adding vital income for their families and energizing the Tutwiler economy.

Anne tells of another woman she treated named Alberta. Alberta said, "Even if you ARE white, I'm gonna hug you!" Anne writes,

> She was in her early 60s, gnarled by years bent picking cotton. I recalled her first visit, 3 weeks before, when her sour look had reflected the toll of incessant pain. All I had done was examine her, diagnose degenerative joint disease and give her an anti-inflammatory pill, requesting that she return. Now she had her strong arms around me, her toothless smile lighting her weathered face. We held close in a moment of communion. Shackles of race, pain and poverty shattered. I had become HER doctor.

Anne stood out because she was not only a woman doctor but also a Catholic nun in a world of Baptists. When she initially wrote to the town leaders, she hadn't told them she was a nun because she didn't come to be a missionary. She said, "I'm not here to make anybody Catholic. The faith of these people is deeper than my own. I get tied up in my work, and I don't think of God as much as I should. God travels with these people."

As of July 2016, the per capita income for Tutwiler was $16,564, with a total population of 3,513. Parts of the community resemble the Depression era, with tin-roofed shacks and other run-down buildings, so the need is still great today.

In 1987 after four years of service, Anne's obligation was up, but she didn't want to leave. "This place has changed me so much. I'm less selfish; material things don't matter anymore. I've learned not to expect instant results. I learned that from the people here, because one of the things poor people do is wait. They wait for everything: food stamps, the doctor, transportation, everything. I receive much more from these people than I could ever give them. I'll leave when they bury me."

Anne lives in a house with three other nuns, all of whom have roles to play at the Tutwiler Clinic. Not only does she work 12 hours a day (with a brief midday nap), she also makes house calls. For several years there was no ambulance service to the

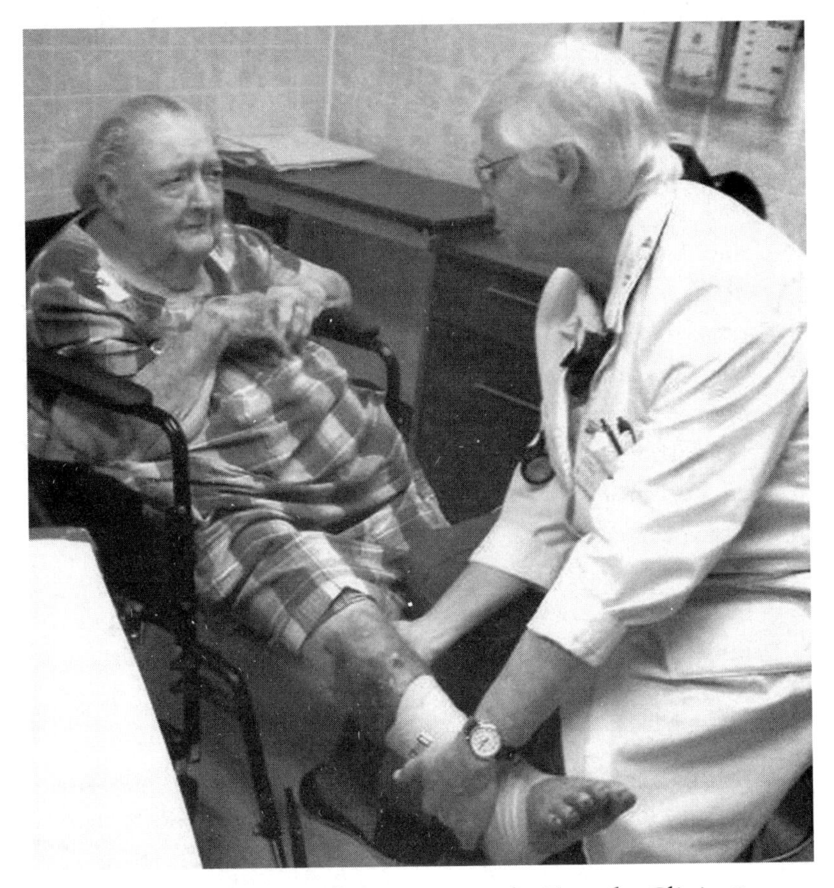

Sister Anne Brooks caring for a patient at the Tutwiler Clinic. *Courtesy of Sister Anne Brooks*

nearest hospital. Many times Sister Anne loaded up a critical house call patient in her old Jeep Wagoneer. While they sped to the emergency room, one sister drove and the other performed CPR in the backseat. They did what they had to do.

THE MISSISSIPPI DELTA

The Mississippi delta is a leaf-shaped area about 200 miles long and 70 miles wide. This flat piece of land wedged between the Mississippi and Yazoo Rivers is some of the most fertile soil in the world. The delta is bordered by Memphis, Tennessee, to the north and Vicksburg, Mississippi, to the south. Cotton planters settled the area in the 1840s, with slaves working the farms up until the Civil War.

The Mississippi delta was a focal point for the American civil rights movement of the 1950s and 1960s. The predominantly African American population battled for voting rights, bringing some change, but in many counties racism still thrives and the area is one of the poorest in the United States. The *Mississippi Labor Market Data* (October 2015) report listed Mississippi's unemployment at an average of 5.9 percent compared to 4.8 percent in the United States. Jobs in agriculture have disappeared as farms have become mechanized, and the population in the delta has decreased by almost half since the 1940s.

In addition to the delta's reputation as the birthplace of the blues, many famous writers have also called the region home: William Faulkner, Eudora Welty, and Tennessee Williams, just to name a few.

Eventually the ambulance would drive to Anne's home, one mile outside of their area. From there she would tell the EMT, "Oh, Joe was going to meet us at my house, but he didn't make it, so we gotta go here, there, around the curve, over by the turnrow. The guys would just sort of laugh and we'd keep going for another 20 miles, and Joe would get the care he needed at the hospital." The EMTs knew they were being hoodwinked but would break all the rules for Anne.

One time a stabbing victim showed up outside her door in the middle of the night. The police were called to help. Not long after, the man who stabbed her patient was brought to Anne's house, too, also with knife wounds. Her neighbor, the Baptist church deacon, came over to protect the nuns with his shotgun while they treated the wounds. The stabber eventually helped his victim dress for the ride to the hospital. Sister Anne has altered the way the community works.

Anne's training as an osteopathic physician leads her to listen to her patients to learn what's really wrong. She doesn't just treat symptoms; she practices a whole-person approach. Osteopathic physicians are trained to understand how the body's systems are interconnected and how each one affects the other. And by treating the whole person, Anne enables the patients to care for themselves.

She believes in the magic of touch, and when she's able to touch a patient without the fear of being sued, she says, there's "a much different connection, because touch can communicate much more than words can." The American Osteopathic Foundation named her the 2012 Physician of the Year.

Many times being a doctor involves more than just practicing medicine. Anne found out early on that there was an immense need for education in Tutwiler. Many of the town's diabetic patients simply didn't know what to eat to keep them healthy, so she tried to teach them or startle them into compliance. She said with a sly smile, "Sometimes, I'll ask them if they've bought their coffin yet."

Tutwiler cried out for emergency food banks, classes for parenting and preventing teenage pregnancy, and play groups for young children. Sister Maureen Delaney directs the Tutwiler Community Education Center. Special events like a Christmas pageant and store, athletic and artistic activities for children, senior citizen offerings, and even a blues band were just a few of the extras that grew out of the Tutwiler Clinic.

When asked how long she would be able to continue working Anne replied, "'Til I croak, I guess." Anne doesn't do things halfway. "We do what we can with what we have," she says. "There's a saying of George Washington Carver that I've always loved: 'Start where you are with what you have, make something of it, and never be satisfied.' And we are not satisfied."

LEARN MORE

The Feminine Touch: Women in Osteopathic Medicine by Thomas A. Quinn (Truman State University Press, 2011)

"Mississippi Delta Health Care" by Saul Gonzalez, *Religion and Ethics NewsWeekly*, September 24, 2010, www.pbs.org/wnet/religionandethics/2010/09/24/september-24-2010-mississippi-delta-health-care/7073/

"Sister Anne Brooks, Doctor and Nun, Practices Without Preaching to the Poor" by Bill Shaw, *People*, March 23, 1987, http://people.com/archive/sister-anne-brooks-doctor-and-nun-practices-without-preaching-to-the-poor-vol-27-no-12/

Jerri Nielsen

Icy Courage

More and more as I am here and see what life really is, I understand that it is not when or how you die but how and if you truly were ever alive.

Jerri Cahill's curiosity led her to dream about places that no one else visited. Duff, her nickname from childhood, was born on March 1, 1952, in Salem, Ohio. She was smart and acrobatic and had a habit of doing her homework upside down, leaning against the wall.

Jerri's mother, who had wanted to be a doctor but became a nurse, told her bedtime science stories. Jerri and her brothers dissected cow eyes and hearts brought home from the butcher and even an octopus, just because they'd never seen one! A career in emergency medicine would be a perfect fit for Jerri. She entered medical school at the Medical College of Ohio in Toledo. Once there she met and married a fellow medical student, Jay Nielsen.

Jerri Nielsen at the South Pole marker, 1999. *Wikimedia Commons*

At first he was a charmer, but their marriage was a rocky one. When they finally divorced, their three children went to live with him. The decision broke Jerri's heart.

Jerri accepted a job as an emergency room physician at a teaching hospital in Cleveland, but without her children she lacked purpose and courage. While leafing through the latest issue of the *Annals of Emergency Medicine*, she spotted an advertisement seeking physicians to work in the US Antarctic Program. The program's purpose was, and is, to support the Antarctic Treaty, which encourages research with other nations. The goal of the program is to study the Antarctic, its ecosystems, and its connections to the rest of the planet. Jerri would work at the South Pole as the only physician, supporting 41 scientists and support personnel.

"I believe in geographic cures," she said in her book, *Ice Bound*. "They allow you to throw all your cards in the air and see where they land, then pick them back up and deal them again. I was ready for a new deal." A few days after reading the ad in October 1998, she interviewed for the position, and soon she was preparing to move to the bottom of the Earth, the Amundsen-Scott South Pole Station.

Before Jerri was allowed to serve as the South Pole doctor, she had to undergo complete physical and mental examinations. She passed them all and there were no concerns. The Antarctic

ANTARCTICA

Antarctica is the coldest, driest, highest, and windiest place on Earth. Summer temperatures rise to an average of −18 degrees Fahrenheit, and winter temperatures dive to −100 degrees Fahrenheit or colder. There are two main areas of Antarctica: West Antarctica, an extension of the Andes Mountains from South America, and East Antarctica, known as Greater Antarctica, covering two-thirds of the continent.

Penguins and seals feed along Greater Antarctica's coasts, and the famous emperor penguin breeds during the frigid Antarctic winters. They travel an average of 50 miles over the ice to breeding colonies.

The Transantarctic Mountains separate the two areas, with large parts of the range buried under the ice. Antarctica's thick ice, covering 98 percent of the continent, makes it the highest continent at an average of 7,500 feet. The peak, at 16,066 feet, is called Vinson Massif, and the lowest point is the Bentley Subglacial Trench in West Antarctica at 8,200 feet below sea level.

Support Associates (ASA) issued her the standard cold-weather gear, including long underwear, fleece jumpsuit and jacket, wind pants, and a goose-down parka. Once winter began Jerri would be stuck there for more than eight months because the fierce weather prohibits airplane landings during all but the summer months. No sunrise, no sunset, total darkness for half of that time. Yet there was something about this that appealed to her.

Jerri flew from Denver to Christchurch, New Zealand, and waited there until the weather was clear enough to continue. This decision would change her life. The Amundsen-Scott Station, where she was to spend most of the next year, was named after Roald Amundsen, a Norwegian, first to the pole in 1911, and Robert Scott from the United Kingdom, second to the pole in 1912.

Roald Amundsen traveled via dogsled and skis and is rumored to have eaten his dogs along the way. Robert Scott reported in his diary when he arrived 35 days after Roald Amundsen on Wednesday, January 17, 1912:

> Camp 69. T. −22°F at start. Night −21°F. The Pole. Yes, but under very different circumstances from those expected. . . . We started at 7:30, none of us having slept much after the shock of our discovery . . . the wind is blowing hard, T. −21°F, and there is that curious damp, cold feeling in the air which chills one to the bone in no time. . . . Great God! This is an awful place and terrible enough for us to have laboured to it without the reward of priority. . . . Now for the run home and a desperate struggle. I wonder if we can do it.

Jerri arrived at the South Pole on November 21, 1998. "I stepped out into the blinding light, into the whitest world under an impossibly blue sky," she later wrote. "My first breaths torched my throat and chilled my lungs. It was cold from another dimension, from an ice planet in a distant galaxy."

Time to get to work. She organized her new supplies and equipment and inventoried what was left from the previous physician. What she found was an antiquated X-ray machine and sterilizer for medical tools, limited antibiotics, and a two-bed hospital called the biomed. She would have to improvise, developing her own X-rays and making some of her own medicines.

She was responsible for the health and dental care of all the scientists and support staff at the pole. She treated everything from frostbite (and there was a lot of that) to injuries sustained while working at the station and illness. Her new home sat on a floor of ice 9,300 feet thick. Several buildings were tucked under a large dome, protecting them from wind but not cold. These two-story structures housed the staff and valuable scientific equipment.

Jerri treated up to 15 patients a day. Band-Aids didn't stick, and wounds healed slowly, even in the summer. But she fit in at the pole and thrived in the environment that required her to think. Her brother Scott sent her an e-mail in preparation for winter saying, "Feel the cold—when winter comes—feel the isolation and solitude—breathe it in, savor this—THIS IS LIFE—this is the edge—the edge is everything."

Forty-one people, or Polies, were left at the pole when the summering crew left on February 15, 1999. They had to be self-sufficient for the next eight months. No one could leave or arrive until the next October. Outside the dome the sky was dark, inside the dome it was −55 degrees Fahrenheit, and just to run between buildings they needed a coat. Hands grew numb almost immediately.

Communication by e-mail or satellite phone is limited to 12 hours a day when the satellite is in range. The food at the station must first be thawed or rehydrated, but there is a greenhouse where some fresh vegetables can be grown in the summer. But the treats all the Polies cherish are slushies made with fresh snow and soda or liquor. Even the ice cream must be warmed in a microwave first before being eaten!

A few months after the last plane dipped its wings, Jerri read in bed. She fingered her chest absentmindedly. Her hand paused, for near the surface of her right breast she felt a "small, hard lump." At first she didn't think too much of it, she had had fibrocystic (small, harmless masses) breasts for most of her life. *That must be what it is, a small cyst*, she thought. Breast cancer was too terrible to even think about. She decided she would watch it for a month and keep her news a secret from the crew.

Jerri was beginning to understand the magnitude of the long winter at the South Pole. She said, "Antarctica was a place so hostile and alien to life, that life sang out, and every small breath was a triumph against nothingness . . . you had to know what you were made of."

John Penney, nicknamed Big John, was Jerri's best friend in the station. She decided to tell him about the lump. He encouraged her to talk to another physician. She sent an e-mail to a radiologist, an old friend. He was alarmed but reassured her that it was probably fine since she had had a mammogram just a few months earlier. She tried to put it out of her mind and continue her mission at the pole. The weight of the bottom of the world was upon her.

She finally wrote to the doctor in charge of the Antarctic medical stations, asking for advice. Surgery on the pole was out; there was no one qualified to help her. They suggested a course of strong antibiotics and steroids to reduce the mass. When that didn't work, the doctors suggested she insert a needle into the mass.

If the fluid was clear, then they could all relax; it was most likely noncancerous. She numbed herself with an ice cube and a lidocaine injection, and directed Paul Kindle, the electrician who had served on the trauma team, to help her. Bad news. They couldn't withdraw any fluid.

The staff in Denver put Jerri in touch with an oncologist at Indiana University, Dr. Kathy Miller. But Jerri was sad at the likelihood of breast cancer, and there would be no way to easily confirm or deny it while at the South Pole. Her friends Big John and Lisa would not let her sink. They forced her up and into the cafeteria to eat.

The team decided to try a needle biopsy, which means removing a sample of the tissue or cells and placing it on a slide for the doctors to read via the computer. They set up a live hookup with the doctors in Denver to coach them through it. Walter Fischel, nicknamed Welder Walt, was named as Jerri's assistant, having been trained as an army medic. Walt and Bill Johnson, the carpentry foreman, practiced sticking needles into vegetables.

Courageously Jerri began the procedure on herself. They raised the head of her bed so she could see, and using ice again to numb the area, she pulled out several tissue samples. Ken Lobe prepared the slides, and then Walt took over to get more tissue. Would the faraway doctors staring at their computers be able to get an accurate read on the sample?

Unfortunately, the doctors could not read the slides because the stain used to see the cells was so out of date. They planned an emergency airdrop to deliver updated slide stains and chemotherapy drugs if cancer was confirmed.

A few weeks later, the day arrived. The enormous plane soared 700 feet above, its cargo door open. Sideways snow had reduced visibility to less than five miles, but station crewmembers set out fire pots to outline the drop zone. The Air Force C-141 Starlifter dropped six packages, two in the first flyby and four in the second. The crew scattered, looking for the dropped packages in −92-degree-Fahrenheit weather and total darkness.

Jerri prepared the biopsy slides, again hoping that this time the doctors halfway around the world could read them. She waited for an answer. If she had breast cancer, what were her odds? Would she have to treat herself at the bottom of the Earth? Would the added time waiting for it to warm up cut her chances of survival?

An e-mail arrived stating the results showed cancer. She couldn't breathe and felt as though someone had kicked her in the stomach. Chemotherapy began immediately and continued for the next three weeks, with one week off.

The newly formed medical staff at the pole named themselves Club Med, and each week they improved at managing Jerri's chemotherapy. Her tumor began to shrink and then grew again. While she lost her hair and shaved her head, plans were formed for a dangerous transport out of the pole before the travel ban ended.

In an e-mail to her physician, Dr. Kathy Miller, Jerri begged for concrete answers about her cancer. She said, "I need to know how to think about my disease so that I can determine if I am even going to try to recover. . . . I don't believe that life can be counted by years or days, but by experience and how you leave the world by the way you live."

Jerri was airlifted out of the South Pole on October 16, 1999, the earliest and coldest ever landing on the South Pole. When she arrived back in the United States, she discovered that her cancer hadn't spread. She elected to have a lumpectomy and was cancer free until August 2005. Jerri died from cancer on June 23, 2009.

Jerri didn't have to fight to become a physician like some women did. Her fight came later when she found the courage to save her own life while living in the most unforgiving place in the world. She became her own patient with grace and bravery. As she said in a note to her parents, she had become "of the ice" where "people are loved for what they give and contribute, their honor, their love and sacrifice."

LEARN MORE

Antarctic Sun, https://antarcticsun.usap.gov

Frozen Secrets: Antarctica Revealed by Sally M. Walker (Carolrhoda Books, 2010)

Ice Scientist: Careers in the Frozen Antarctic by Sara Latta (Enslow, 2009)

United States Antarctic Program, www.usap.gov

Kathy Magliato

A Persistent Heart

My life's work has been about giving people time. Time to live and, when it is their time, time to die.

Mopping floors. Cleaning toilets. Collecting trash. Each janitorial shift that 16-year-old Kathy Magliato worked at the nursing home was a chance to witness medicine in action. The first floor of the home housed the sickest residents. Most of the time the nurses took control, so Kathy observed them. But when a doctor was called to the facility, she made an effort to clean that room at that exact moment, just so she could watch.

Their garb, equipment, even their expressions showed the differences between the doctors and nurses. As a young girl from a small town in upstate New York, Kathy had always assumed she couldn't become a doctor because she was a girl—until one day when her new boss walked in. Her name was Pat and she was the *woman* in charge of the janitorial service. Kathy

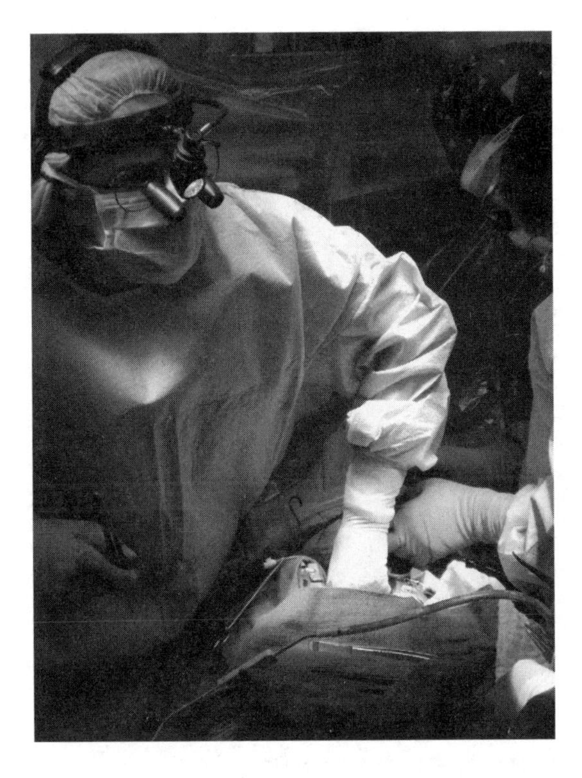

Dr. Kathy Magliato performing heart surgery. *Courtesy of Kathy Magliato*

thought, *If Pat is a woman and a boss, couldn't I work in a man's world, too? As a doctor?*

At first Kathy kept the dream to herself. But when she finally told her parents, she felt the power behind their push—just like their push of her bike during her first solo ride without training wheels. She'd looked back as she sped down the hill. She was on her own, but there at the top of the hill stood her family, supporting her from a distance.

Her mother said, "Your parents give you two things; one is roots and the other is wings." But Kathy's childhood wasn't all bike rides. She worked the family's orchard for extra income, and often when there was no meat for dinner, her mom made "gravy bread," a piece of bread with gravy on it. Most kids in the area did not go to college. When Kathy toured Union College in Schenectady, New York, she was impressed. At first studying biochemistry, she nearly failed out. School had come easy to her in high school, but college was different. Once she figured out that she had to quit partying and work harder, her grades improved.

She graduated with honors, but medical school applications did not go as planned. She didn't get admitted the first time. She retook the Medical College Admission Test (MCAT) and was accepted at Albany Medical Center in New York. Later she transferred to Case Western Reserve University in Cleveland, Ohio. Coincidentally it was the same school Emily Blackwell and Marie Zakrzewska had graduated from in the 1850s.

Kathy chose surgery as her specialty when she graduated from medical school in 1990. At that time female general surgery physicians were rare. And as of 2010, women made up only 15.4 percent of all general surgery physicians. Kathy would have to become "one of the boys."

One of the first things she learned in residency was finding a midway point between tough and kind. The chief resident at

THE HIPPOCRATIC OATH

The Hippocratic oath is an oath taken by almost all doctors and is one of the oldest binding documents in history. Doctors swear to treat the sick to the best of their ability and to share their knowledge with those who come after them. They also pledge to protect patient privacy, and treat the patient with kindness and sympathy, understanding that these attributes are sometimes more important than the "surgeon's knife or the chemist's drug." In 1928 only about 24 percent of medical school students took the oath, while nearly 100 percent do today.

Metro County Hospital in Cleveland told the group, "If you treat all of your patients like they are your family, you will always do right by the patient." Kathy believed this was the best way to live up to and go beyond the Hippocratic oath.

In order to fit in with "the boys," Kathy adopted an imaginary "full-metal jacket." Wearing it, she would be able to face all challenges, but an event during her general surgical residency forced her to rethink this armor. Cancer had invaded a patient's shoulder, and removing the arm was the only course of treatment. As Kathy assisted during the surgery, the head surgeon said, "Hold the arm and pull."

Was she really going to pull off this poor woman's arm? What would this patient feel like without it? How could she ever hug anyone again? Kathy did as she was told. She gripped the woman's limb and tucked it under her own armpit. She leaned away for both leverage and to turn her back on the grim surgery. The surgeon kept calling it *the* arm, not *her* arm. He had to be tough, so he donned his "full-metal jacket," just as she had.

As she held the woman's arm, she recited the periodic table in her head. Anything to get her mind away from her task. Suddenly Kathy pitched forward, detached from the woman yet still holding her arm. As she placed the now-untethered body part in a specimen bin, she was grateful for her armor. Even though she had worried about her patient, she realized later that she was able to put this woman's troubles behind her much too quickly. Kathy decided she should loosen her "full-metal jacket" to let in a little kindness.

From that day forward, she has attempted to walk the tightrope between tough doctor and caring physician. One of her general surgery mentors, Dr. Kaymen, said to her, "In order to be not just a good surgeon, but a great surgeon, you need the eye of an eagle, the heart of a lion, and the hand of a lady."

Balancing feelings was one thing; remaining calm under pressure was another. One time as a resident, a nurse had summoned her into a cardiac surgical case. It is common, according to Kathy, to be yelled at, directed, and pushed around as an intern. An intern wasn't a true member of the surgical team, just an extra body whose only goal was to do no harm.

The patient was in trouble. There was so much blood that Kathy had to be careful not to slip on the operating floor. The surgeon in charge, Dr. Netter, said, "Grab the heart and hold it steady so I can get a few stitches in the hole we have here."

Kathy did as she was told. She reached in and closed her hand around the struggling heart. As soon as she embraced it, she fell in love. How cool would it be if she could touch the human heart every day for the rest of her life? What an honor. What a privilege.

As she moved on in her training, she hit one obstacle after another. Tactless comments from the male doctors about whether she could handle the job invaded her mind. There was one instance, after Kathy assisted on a successful surgery, when the attending physician told the family what a good job Kathy had done and then slapped her hard on the butt, like a quarterback might do to a receiver after a touchdown. The entire waiting room noticed. Kathy fled,

Dr. Kathy Magliato.
Courtesy of Kathy Magliato

pretending to answer a page, and took her anger out on every stall door of the women's room. She didn't report the incident, fearing it could damage her career.

Despite such incidents, Kathy never let this male doctor, or any others, stop her progress. She has had to fight the battle so that other women could follow in her footsteps. She considers herself a path-paver, complete with potholes. At a talk at the 2013 Women's Leadership Conference at Mount St. Mary's College, Kathy summed up her fight: "If you have a goal and someone tells you 'no,' go and find someone who tells you 'yes.' Part of being a leader is not just having passion, but being able to communicate that passion to others."

In 1998 Kathy finished her training in cardiothoracic surgery. She pursued further training at the University of Pittsburgh Medical Center in the heart/lung fellowship program. All surgeons have to be respectful of time, but the transplant surgeon is under the ultimate pressure. In order for the patient to have a chance, the team has to remove the heart from the donor, preserve and package it for transport, and sew it into the recipient's chest in less than four hours.

The biggest problem for heart transplant surgeries today is locating enough donated hearts. Heart disease has increased, and today about 5.1 million people in the United States have heart failure and about half of those die within five years.

Right now almost 4,000 people are waiting for new hearts. Other organs are transplanted, too, and when one person dies many people can be saved. As Kathy puts it, "What if the recipient of that lung goes on to find the cure for cancer?"

Kathy's mission in writing her memoir, *Heart Matters*, was not only to tell her story of becoming a heart surgeon but also to talk about women's heart health. "My job, the way I see it, is to educate women how to prevent a disease that is 80%

preventable. You can't change your age or your genetic composition but all the other risk factors, smoking, diabetes, hypertension, obesity, lifestyle, those we can all do something about."

Heart disease is the number one killer of women, taking more lives than all forms of cancer combined. The American Heart Association estimates one woman in the United States dies from heart disease every 60 seconds. But the human heart's best quality is its persistence, beating an average of 80 times per minute and 100,000 times per day.

Kathy operates in a 55-degree room; the colder the better. It's an intimidating environment filled with whooshing and beeping machinery. She listens to rock and roll when she feels it will enhance her performance. But "sometimes it's kind of nice when it's just quiet."

Stamina is important, so in order to last for an 18-hour surgery, she eats and uses the bathroom prior to operating. She wears a high-powered headlamp for extra light, as well as special magnifying glasses that allow her to stitch miniscule blood vessels. "The operating room feels like its own living, breathing entity. But it's also very complex. Everybody has a job there and everybody knows their job. We're only there to serve the needs of the patient."

The first incision is always made perfectly down the middle of the patient's chest because she believes that what you see on the outside is mirrored on the inside. When the first incision is complete, she takes one moment to touch the beating heart—her secret with the patient on a "very privileged journey."

Kathy believes the amount of focus she brings into the operating room every day is critical. "I'm a big believer in having focus within your life. When I'm in the operating room I never make an incision greater than the length from the tip of my pinky to the tip of my thumb. Imagine an incision that big, and now imagine yourself standing over that incision for 6 or 8 or 10 or 14 hours every day. It takes a very powerful amount of focus to be a surgeon. And that focus permeates my life."

Along with this focus, she says you must have clear-cut goals. "I don't even get out of bed in the morning without a plan A, and then I make sure I've got a plan B and one for every letter of the alphabet." In addition, to be a surgeon she says you must have passion. It is the glue to hold the hard work, the perseverance, and the courage together, all of which are important in health care.

Kathy is raising two boys with her husband, Nick, a liver transplant surgeon. With a successful thoracic surgery practice in California, Kathy decides on a daily basis where to put the fulcrum, or hinge, so that she can balance between work and life without extreme swings. She believes in juggling work and life, and she says, "I'm a really good juggler."

LEARN MORE

Heart Matters: A Memoir of a Female Heart Surgeon by Kathy E. Magliato, (Three Rivers, 2010)

The Human Body: The Story of How We Protect, Repair, and Make Ourselves Stronger by H. P. Newquist (Viking, 2015)

"Map of the Human Heart" by Kate Hudec, NOVA, www.pbs.org/wgbh/nova/body/map-human-heart.html

Bonnie Simpson Mason

Taking It to the Nth Dimension

It's a team effort. None of us have done it alone.

Sixteen-year-old Bonnie Simpson had set her sights on becoming cheerleader captain for her senior year. But first she had to get through spring tryouts and make the team. The high school gym was loud and full of other girls; competition would be fierce. Sliding her left leg down to perform the splits, she felt a pop just under her left hip. Searing pain. Unrelenting pain.

The athletic trainer rushed over. She determined that Bonnie had suffered a significant hamstring injury. Over the summer, the physical therapist worked with her. With hot whirlpool baths and stretching exercises, she began to get better. The physical therapy was working, and Bonnie was intrigued. Could physical therapy be her future career?

She said to her mom, "I want to be a physical therapist." To which her mother replied, "Why not be the physician that tells

Dr. Bonnie Mason.
Gary Landsman, courtesy of Bonnie Mason

the physical therapist what to do." Dr. Bonnie Mason said, "The decision to be a physician was made, it was that simple. It was just that simple."

Bonnie's mother, already immersed in a man's world as a construction engineer, became a living role model. Bonnie describes her mother as tenacious, and as a young girl Bonnie took note. Her parents created a world in which Bonnie and her sister knew they couldn't fail. Bonnie's sister, a physician specializing in child and adolescent psychiatry, also guided her.

Bonnie was born in 1970 in El Paso, Texas. Her parents met at Howard University, where her father was working toward a PhD in physics and her mother toward a degree in architecture. In the midst of his PhD candidacy, her father was drafted and sent to Fort Bliss, Texas, ultimately to serve in Vietnam.

While he was gone, the young family moved in with Bonnie's great aunt and uncle in Atlanta. Uncle John (Dr. John E. Hall Sr.) was the first African American pediatrician in Atlanta. Bonnie didn't have to look far for a medical role model.

Atlanta in the 1970s was full of progressive energy. Leaders such as Maynard Jackson, the first African American mayor of Atlanta; Benjamin E. Mays, a mentor to Martin Luther King Jr. and president of Morehouse College from 1940 to 1967; and Coretta Scott King, widow of Martin Luther King and often referred to as the first lady of the African American civil rights movement, helped Atlanta become the hub for middle-class black America.

Bonnie couldn't help but be inspired by the "energy of a positive African American community that expected that you'd do well in school." After college she enrolled at Morehouse School of Medicine and assumed she would excel. She had done well in the physical sciences like chemistry and physics, how hard could the rest of the subjects be?

Pharmacology is the study of how drugs affect the body and what they do to cure and prevent disease. Bonnie found herself getting behind in pharmacology, but she wanted to figure it out on her own. By the time she asked her friend Kendall Jones for help, though, it was too late.

To keep her full scholarship, she needed a 3.0 grade point average. After pharmacology she posted a 2.99 grade point average. She went to Dean Angela Franklin's office with a racing heart and pleaded on her knees.

But Dr. Franklin looked at Bonnie with a straight face and said, "Unfortunately a 2.99 does not equal a 3.0." Because Bonnie had let her ego get in the way, she lost her scholarship and is still paying down her student loans. Lesson learned, she said. "We have to ask for the help we need."

Bonnie's first encounter with a cadaver in medical school was difficult, too. She had to leave the room because she felt sick. She says, "Don't let a one-time experience determine whether we can or can't do something. Give it one more try."

Bonnie graduated from medical school and entered into a general surgical residency at the University of California, Los Angeles, and later an orthopedic residency at Howard University Hospital in Washington, DC.

A common assumption in orthopedics is that you have to do a lot of lifting. Were women simply not strong enough? But Bonnie said, "Mastering orthopedic surgery requires more brain than brawn; some of the most capable orthopedic surgeons in the country are women who stand less than 5'4" tall and weigh less than 125 pounds." She continued, "Orthopedics was traumatic more from a female perspective than an African American perspective. You know in this specialty, you're an odd duck being female."

Bonnie didn't think twice about entering the predominantly white male field of orthopedics. All she had to do was think, "OK, well, my mom did it (as a construction engineer), and she did it 20 years before I did."

Near the end of her fourth year of residency, Bonnie noticed an achiness in the balls of both feet. Being a southern girl, she'd been trained to look professional and wore skirts and heels every day. She thought, *It must be the heels*, and wore them less frequently. Bonnie had risen to chief resident. It was finally her "chance to be at the operating table with the knife and do the surgery." She wouldn't let a little foot pain get in the way of all she had worked for.

Then one day after a particularly long operation, Bonnie experienced more pain. She said, "It felt like someone had shoved a knife into my right shoulder. It was a burning pain lasting for a couple of hours." During the next few months, other random symptoms appeared, and the most serious of these was motor weakness. She went to the emergency room, where they performed several tests.

She was diagnosed with rheumatoid arthritis, a debilitating disease affecting many joints and muscles. The regimen of strong drugs and missed work days was almost more traumatic to Bonnie than having the disease. She had to compromise her work ethic, giving people an excuse to criticize her.

Bonnie had been accepted into a prestigious hand surgery fellowship in New York City. Fellowships last one to two years and occur after residencies, allowing the physicians additional training. When the doctors were unable to get her rheumatoid arthritis under control, she was forced to give up her spot. She joined Grant Orthopaedic Bone and Joint Surgeons and also served as the group's chief financial officer.

Rheumatoid arthritis viciously attacked her right elbow, and because Bonnie is right handed, surgery became more and more difficult. She could still see patients in the clinic, but it was difficult for her. "I'm a surgeon, and I like active hands. I need that instant gratification, but when you're done, oh the bone was broken and now it is fixed."

Instead of being angry at having to give up her active practice, her mentor, Dr. Richard Grant, advised her to react on a spiritual level. He told her, "'If you read the psalms, David is pissed off at God, and God wants an honest relationship,'" so, Bonnie concluded, "I needed to talk to Him."

This conversation was liberating. She was able to process the loss of her career by being honest with herself. She began to reinvent herself.

But what could Bonnie do now with the knowledge and experience she had worked so hard for? Community service intrigued her, and she saw education as an opportunity. "My parents were living examples of giving back, even with working hard and raising two girls."

She taught simple science at elementary schools, and at Morehouse School of Medicine she gave clinical lectures to first-year medical students in the gross anatomy lab. She also sought out orthopedic inventions and connected with Zimmer, Inc., which creates joint replacement technologies to restore mobility.

Bonnie has had many influential mentors, such as Dr. Claudia Thomas, the first African American woman to become an orthopedic surgeon. "She showed me that my dream of becoming an orthopedic surgeon could become a reality. She conveyed the realities of gender inequity in orthopedics and demonstrated strategies for successfully maneuvering into and through the field."

At about this time, Bonnie met her husband, a physician in internal medicine. Together with her many mentors, Bonnie's husband and children have been instrumental in her accomplishments.

In 2005 Bonnie founded Nth Dimensions, which seeks to expose women and minorities to orthopedic surgery. Mentoring is an important key to these successes. She wanted the name of her nonprofit to be math and science based. The use of the *n* signals an infinite number of possibilities, or in this case an "infinite number of dimensions."

The overall goal of the nonprofit is to address the gaps in health care in the United States by increasing diversity, understanding, and trust. "A higher level of trust equals better compliance, better outcome, and increased access to medical care."

Nth Dimensions provides medical students and residents with scholarships, internships, and grants.

In 2005 a young woman from South Georgia was attending the Medical College of Georgia. Tamara Huff was one of only two female African American students in the school at that time. She approached Bonnie at the Student National Medical Association's national meeting and asked for guidance on getting into Nth Dimension's summer internship.

Tamara was paired with Dr. Mary O'Connor, an orthopedic surgeon practicing at the Mayo Clinic in Jacksonville, Florida.

THE PERRY INITIATIVE

Like Nth Dimensions, the Perry Initiative is vested with mentoring and teaching female high school, college, and medical school students in orthopedic surgery, adding engineering to the mix. It was named for Dr. Jacquelin Perry, who was one of the first female orthopedic surgeons in the United States.

Jacquelin used ultrasound studies to trace the nerve pathways through all of the 28 major muscles in each leg. Through detailed photographs she was able to analyze walking, running, and climbing patterns and became known as a gait, or walking, expert. She also developed new surgical techniques for polio patients after they had been released from iron lungs. She died in 2013 at the age of 94.

The Perry Initiative, founded in 2009 by mechanical engineer Dr. Jenni Buckley and orthopedic surgeon Dr. Lisa Lattanza, teaches young women about the close relationship between orthopedics and engineering. These two disciplines work seamlessly in developing and improving implants for broken bones and worn-out joints. Through the outreach programs, more than 1,000 women each year are exposed to engineering and orthopedic surgery techniques.

Dr. Tamara Huff came to Bonnie three years later and spoke of her challenges; how she doubted whether she'd be successful and whether she fit into the residency program where she had matched. Could she handle it? Bonnie says, "You have to

Dr. Bonnie Mason receiving the 2015 American Academy of Orthopaedic Surgeons Diversity Award. *Courtesy of Bonnie Mason*

balance this internal conflict; saying 'I can't do it' with 'yes, I can.'"

Bonnie was the honoree of the 2015 American Academy of Orthopaedic Surgeons (AAOS) Diversity Award. She said regarding her company, "I wanted to create pathways for this information to get to the students coming behind me to really usher through the next generation of orthopedic surgeons as leaders."

When asked about advice she'd like to give young women, she says, "Think about the areas that you're good at and everybody's good at something. Identify a void and fill it. See a problem and create a solution. Especially if you can align that with something you like to do, you're right on target."

LEARN MORE

American Academy of Orthopaedic Surgeons, www.aaos.org

Nth Dimensions, www.nthdimensions.org

The Perry Initiative, http://perryinitiative.org

Adele Levine

A Leap of Faith

Regardless of a patient's true motives to get out of bed, I always applaud on the inside. That's what physical therapy is all about. To get them out of bed.

When she was in her twenties, Adele Levine jumped from job to job. "I always felt like a dummy and never thought I would actually do anything more than wait tables at a diner or landscaping."

But one night in a bookstore, Adele spotted a *US News and World Report* display highlighting the best jobs for the 21st century. "Physical therapy was in the top 10. I didn't know anything about physical therapy, but it sounded more appealing than actuary science and accounting. But the more I read about it, the more it seemed like it might be a good fit for me because I enjoy learning about the body and how the body heals itself, and I like working with people to solve a problem."

Adele Levine with her dog, Howie. *Courtesy of Adele Levine*

Adele had a job with a publishing company but didn't think it was going anywhere. She called her decision to go back to school for physical therapy a leap of faith.

Adele was born in St. Louis, Missouri, in 1970 and raised by strict parents who didn't let her get away with much. Every morning, including summers, according to Adele, her father, who had been an infectious disease officer in the Public Health Service, woke her at 0600, military time for 6:00 AM. "If I didn't get immediately out of bed and he had to knock on my door a second time, I'd be instantly grounded. Similarly, if I was even one minute late for my curfew, I was grounded. My dad would be waiting for me in the kitchen, standing directly underneath the clock." Yet they instilled in her a work ethic and strong sense of responsibility.

Adele moved 11 times as a child. She always felt a little rootless, but since then she's been able to adjust to all kinds of situations. She says, "You could drop me on the moon and I would be just fine."

The physical therapy school application demanded that she complete all the pre-med coursework, which seemed okay at the time, just in case she would change her mind and enter medical, dental, or nursing school. "I remember the day I got my acceptance letter. The first person I called was my grandma. She was ecstatic and told me over the phone, 'Everyone told me not to get my hopes up—but I knew you'd get in!'"

Adele calls physical therapy school the hardest endurance race of her life. Studying gross anatomy, she spent hours every day in the cadaver lab dissecting donor bodies layer by layer. She recalls one particular event: "The cadaver lab was in an office building attached to the hospital, but most of the office workers didn't know it was there. I remember leaving the lab once to

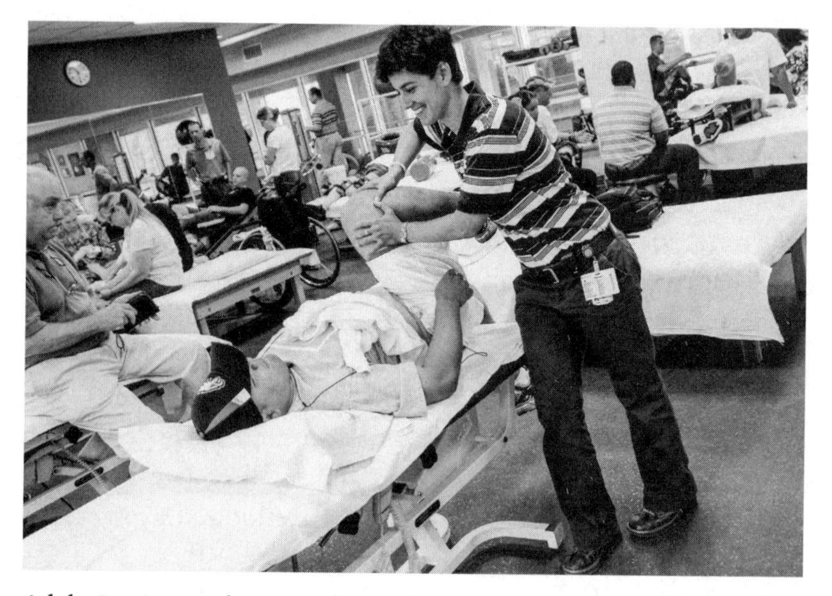

Adele Levine with a patient in the amputee clinic. *Courtesy of Adele Levine*

get a cup of coffee and got trapped between floors in the elevator with some administrator who went completely crazy when she caught a whiff of me in my lab coat stained with human remains. She literally tried to claw her way out of the elevator while I stood in the corner and reviewed flash cards."

After graduation and a few short-term physical therapy jobs, Adele moved into a one-bedroom apartment across the street from Walter Reed Army Medical Center. When her new landlord asked if she had a job there, she had to say no. She didn't yet have a job and hadn't even considered Walter Reed. But since the hospital was right across the street from her apartment, she might as well apply. She had always appreciated easy commutes.

Adele got the job, and in 2007 she walked into the rehabilitation room at Walter Reed Army Medical Center Amputee Clinic. Amputees struggling to return to a normal life groaned and sweated inside the glassed-in gym that reminded Adele of a fishbowl.

The injured arrived at Walter Reed within three days of their injuries. Surgery for most happened immediately to repair and clean their wounds. Physical therapy began straightaway, even while the patients were loaded up with drugs and tubes.

The circus-like atmosphere in the fishbowl had one big goal: getting the amputees moving. She said, "It was so important to get a patient down to the MATC [Military Advanced Training Center] as soon as possible. We needed to light that fire."

The physical therapists treated as many as 100 patients each week. Most had been injured by explosions in Afghanistan or Iraq, some missing one limb and a few missing all four. After many surgeries, the patient would be ready for a prosthetic—a metal replacement limb.

They began on "stubbies," one-foot-tall prosthetic legs without a knee. If patients fell over, they would have a shorter, safer fall. After they graduated to full-size prosthetic legs, complete with tennis shoes, or stiletto heels in the case of one female patient, they would learn to walk as smoothly as possible.

One patient of Adele's was a young man named Jasper Pigeon (his name has been changed to protect his privacy). He was an "AK" (above-the-knee amputee) on one leg and had lost half his foot on the other. Jasper was understandably angry at his circumstances and lashed out frequently. Adele and Jasper had one thing in common: they both liked intense workouts after which the fatigue was so overwhelming, all you could do was collapse. Adele had felt that exhaustion in the past, training as a triathlete and now as a long-distance swimmer, but long hours in the amputee clinic left her with little energy to enter the pool.

Because Jasper's injury was so high up on his thigh, his prosthetic didn't fit like it should. He complained to Adele that he was getting fat, and all he wanted to do was "get smoked," meaning totally exhausted from a workout. Adele wondered if swimming would help Jasper.

Adele said, "We learned some surprising things: It is impossible for a person who is missing both legs to sink; you can do back flips off the side of the pool using just your arms to spring you into the air; and even if you are a triple amputee missing both legs and an arm, you can pull yourself easily and gracefully a half-dozen times back and forth across the pool with your one good arm."

At Walter Reed Adele thought she would be getting easy hours and little stress. She was wrong. Long hours dealing with devastating injuries wore her down and caused dreams full of amputees, but they weren't soldiers. They were people she loved; her parents and sister. Even when people were watching, she would imagine seeing strangers as amputees. "My friends looked at the person's face, and probably their butt, but I was singularly focused on legs and arms, straining to see the telltale sign of a prosthesis."

The amputee clinic celebrated everything, even the anniversary of that terrible day that brought the amputee into Walter Reed. Because they had survived, it was called the patient's "Alive Day."

And everyone—patients and therapists alike—laughed as much as possible. Even the amputees themselves joked, calling each other "ugly stump" or wearing T-shirts that read MARINE—SOME ASSEMBLY REQUIRED.

Adele dealt with both the physical and mental status of her patients. Explosions did more than ruin limbs; they could ruin your brain, too. Traumatic brain injury wasn't always apparent.

While working on his balance, one patient was to tap an orange cone, then step over it. He tapped it, then stepped to the side instead of over. Or he tapped it and just quit. His brain

TRAUMATIC BRAIN INJURY

Traumatic brain injury occurs when the head comes in contact with something else—another person or object. This injury can be severe or mild, with effects lasting from a few days to the rest of your life. Loss of memory, impaired thinking, or changes in vision or hearing can all be symptoms. In the case of soldiers, the injury is often a result of an explosive device injuring not only their brain but limbs as well. During the fighting in Iraq and Afghanistan, there were thought to have been between 48,000 and 360,000 traumatic brain injuries, most of them concussions.

injury made it difficult to focus on more than one step to the exercise. Adele didn't get flustered with this soldier, she just repeated the exercise. Tap and step over. Tap and step over.

Amputees with new prosthetics first practiced on parallel bars, catching themselves with their arms if they fell. They graduated to negotiate obstacles like curbs, stairs, and uneven terrain. For speed and additional strength, they would tow their therapist around the clinic using resistance bands. And then the big day arrived. The soldier was strapped to the table wearing his new legs. The table was tilted up. Families snapped pictures as he stood again for the first time!

Adele considers the book she wrote about her experiences, *Run, Don't Walk: The Curious and Chaotic Life of a Physical Therapist Inside Walter Reed Army Medical Center*, one of her greatest

WALTER REED GENERAL HOSPITAL

Built in 1909, Walter Reed General Hospital was named after a young army doctor and researcher who discovered that yellow fever was transmitted by mosquitos. The hospital grew during World War I, increasing in the number of beds from 80 to 2,500 in a few months and eventually rose to 10 stories. Walter Reed Army Medical Center served the nation through World Wars I and II, the Korean War, Vietnam, Iraq, and Afghanistan, in total for more than 102 years. Walter Reed closed its doors and combined with the National Naval Medical Center in 2011 to become the Walter Reed National Military Medical Center in Bethesda, Maryland.

accomplishments. It took her two years to write, and at first she didn't think anyone took her or her writing seriously. "I remember thinking how crazy it was that I was at Random House, but sad that I couldn't enjoy being there because I was sure that in about ten minutes I was going to be tossed across the lobby by an angry group of editors for wasting their time. So I was completely surprised to walk into a conference room and experience what felt like a ticket-tape parade. Everyone was excited about my book. They were shaking my hand and patting me on the back. It was not at all what I thought was going to happen."

During those eight-and-a-half years at Walter Reed, Adele learned that you have to go into medicine because you want to work with all types of people. She says,

> I like physical therapy because I work with old people, young people, rich people, poor people. I see all sorts of injuries. . . . Because I wrote a book about my experience working in an Army hospital I frequently hear from PT students who tell me they only want to work with active duty military patients because they just want to work with 'motivated people.' I find that very disappointing. You can find motivated people and unmotivated people everywhere. And everyone is deserving of good medical care—not just professional athletes and soldiers, but old grandmas who take the bus, and people who just had the bad fortune to get sick.

Today Adele and her partner, Ashley, are raising two boys. She calls them the greatest loves of her life and only wishes she had had them earlier. She currently works as a physical therapist in Maryland. She still has an easy commute but has better hours.

LEARN MORE

American Physical Therapy Association, www.apta.org

A Career as a Physical Therapist by Therese Harasymiw (Rosen Publications, 2011)

Run, Don't Walk: The Curious and Chaotic Life of a Physical Therapist Inside Walter Reed Army Medical Center by Adele Levine (Avery, 2014)

Sherrie Ballantine-Talmadge

Back on the Field!

Graduating from college and medical school—these are two of the happiest days of my life. Getting my medical degree was proof that dreams come true and you can accomplish anything if you dream, believe in that dream, and work hard.

The 1984 Winter Olympics in Sarajevo, Bosnia, kept seven-year-old Sherrie glued to the television. She focused in on the figure skater's grace and athleticism, and said, "Wow, that's perfect for me."

Over the next year or so, Sherrie pleaded with her mother to become a figure skater. Money was tight, and figure skating is an expensive sport. One day Sherrie pulled the yellow pages out of the cabinet and looked up skates and rinks. Her mother finally gave in and drove her to the rink.

Dr. Sherrie Ballantine-Talmadge at the University of Colorado Sports Medicine and Performance Center, Boulder, Colorado. *Courtesy of Sherrie Ballantine-Talmadge*

A few years later in seventh grade, Sherrie Ballantine laced up her figure skates and stepped out on the ice to begin her warm-up. Figure skating had become her whole life; leaving school early or waking before the sun for ice time, spending every available minute practicing the sport she loved.

As a lefty Sherrie had to skate against the majority of other skaters who were righties, and sometimes she jumped closer to the boards. But she had gotten used to taking off on combinations and usually knew exactly where the boards were. This time something went wrong. She leapt into the air to perform a double lutz, double toe loop combination. She landed the first jump but realized too late the closeness of the boards. Crashing into the boards, instant shoulder pain seized her. She couldn't move her arm.

Dr. Sherrie Ballantine-Talmadge was born Sherrie Lynn Ballantine in Winfield, Illinois, a suburb of Chicago, on June 15, 1977. Her father, Fred, was a World War II veteran and professional baseball player, first with the Boston Red Sox and later with the Detroit Tigers. Athletics were everything in her childhood, and she participated in pretty much every sport. "The best gift my parents gave me was the opportunity to explore."

Her parents divorced early in Sherrie's life, and her mother, Darlene, raised her as single mom, making a living as a school bus driver. Sherrie says, "I wouldn't be who I am today without her."

At first her shoulder injury was misdiagnosed as a sprain, and she was frustrated because she wasn't getting any better. Skating was everything to her: "This was my life, it was a big deal." Her mother took her to Dr. Richard Dominguez, cofounder of Wheaton Orthopaedics in Illinois, and things began to change. He correctly diagnosed a growth plate fracture, or broken shoulder.

He treated her like a whole person, listening to her concerns and helping her overcome them. When he tragically died in a car accident in 1995, his funeral was a testament to his legacy. The police were needed to control the crowds arriving to pay their respects, and he was remembered by his coworkers on the Wheaton Orthopaedics website: "His pioneering spirit, medical expertise, and spiritual strength provide all of us with a great legacy." To this day Sherrie considers him her first mentor.

Dr. Daniel Davidson, doctor of osteopathic medicine, took Sherrie's case and stepped in as her new guide. This was the first time Sherrie was introduced to osteopathic medicine. Daniel Davidson also treated Sherrie as a whole person and introduced the concept of osteopathic manipulative medicine (commonly known as OMM).

Sherrie's love of athletics and intrigue with the human body steered her toward a career in orthopedics and sports medicine like her two mentors. When it came time to apply to medical schools, she only applied to osteopathic medical schools because she believed the treatments had made a difference in her healing. Doctors of osteopathic medicine receive extensive training in the musculoskeletal system, which Sherrie knew would help in her sports medicine practice.

She set up rotations with several orthopedic surgeons. When one was unable to attend a family function because of work, she realized how much he missed because of the demanding orthopedic surgery practice. He and his wife had recently hired a nanny, and it was she who took care of their children a large part of each day. The doctor told her, "Sherrie, I'm just not around that much."

Sherrie realized the sacrifices she would have to make to become an orthopedic surgeon like her mentors. She had recently married her college sweetheart, Brian Talmadge, and knew someday they would want to raise a family. Sherrie had

SPORTS MEDICINE

Sports medicine is a specialty centered on treating injuries suffered by both professional and everyday athletes. It was first recognized as a science during the 1928 Olympic Games. Physicians and trainers joined to form the International Federation of Sports Medicine (FIMS), which exists to protect the health and well-being of those involved in exercise and sports.

According to the Centers for Disease Control and Prevention, 7.1 million Americans suffer exercise and sports injuries each year. And in children aged 12 to 17 sports-related injuries are the leading cause of emergency room visits. Sports medicine researchers look into ways both to prevent and treat such serious injuries as concussions, traumatic brain injury, and spinal injuries. The most common injuries sports medicine physicians treat are muscle strains and tears.

an epiphany, saying to herself, *Wouldn't the kids be better with me around?* She decided to specialize in family and sports medicine and hasn't looked back.

Early in her career, she became an assistant team physician for Northwestern University Athletics, helping to care for nearly 500 student athletes. Soccer player Meredith Finsand was one college athlete Sherrie treated. She said, "Dr. Ballantine once described my knees as looking like a 'Spanish moss tree' because my cartilage was hanging in all sorts of directions and getting yanked by my patella every time my knees bent. I was on and off the field a little too often. Every time I talked she actually looked at me and listened to what I had to say and was trying to figure out a way to get me back on the soccer field. She really cared about the athlete's pain and how to fix it."

Sherrie recalled another Northwestern University athlete. Fallon Fitzpatrick was a freshman swimmer from Florida who had been sick with a fever and sore throat for more than two weeks but tested negative for both strep and mononucleosis. One day she passed out and was rushed to the hospital. First she was diagnosed with pneumonia and later with the rare disease Lemierre's syndrome. Fallon had no one in town to rely on other than Sherrie.

Lemierre's syndrome begins with a throat infection. The infection spreads rapidly through the bloodstream and can be extremely serious if not caught early. As Fallon recovered she wondered about her swimming career. It was so much a part of who she was. Could she come back and compete again?

A sports medicine physician is charged with the challenge of helping those injured or ill return to the sport they love. Sherrie understood Fallon because of her own experience as a figure skater. She herself had returned after her broken shoulder and knew that she could help.

After a year of rehab, Fallon did in fact return to the pool as a Division I swimmer, and she finished out her career. At least in part because of the care Sherrie gave her, she's now in training to be a nurse practitioner. Sherrie said, "I have a passion for helping young females and believe in payback mentorship, just as I was mentored. And now she will pay it forward."

Two years ago she was given the opportunity to join a family and sports medicine practice in Colorado. "Making the decision to leave and move to Colorado was one of the hardest things I've ever done. I left family and friends as well as comfort and security behind." She and her husband have always loved the outdoors, especially the mountains. "It was the right choice," she says, "a step of maturity to take everything I've learned and put it all together."

Colorado University Sports Medicine and Performance Center recently opened a state-of-the-art treatment center. They see many types of patients, but one injury that many athletes encounter is concussion, and Sherrie is focused on concussion management. According to the American College of Sports Medicine, "A concussion is an injury to the brain where force causes the brain to move within the skull. A person does not need to lose consciousness or have

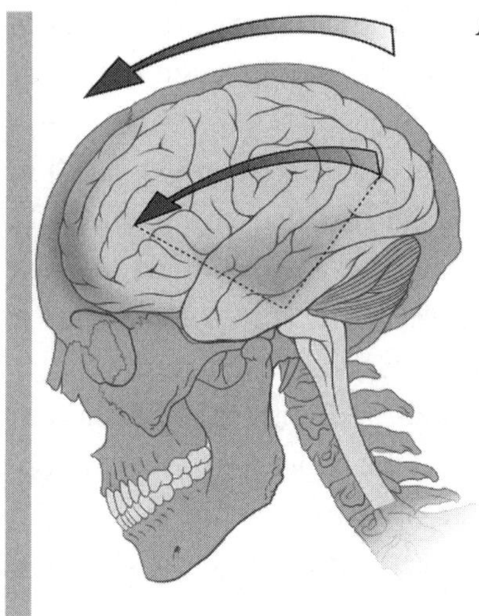

The forces on the brain in a concussion. *Wikimedia Commons*

hit their head to suffer a concussion. Hits to the head—against another person, a ball, or the ground—are a common cause."

Thirteen-year-old soccer goalie Amelia Simmons tracked the opposing forward sprinting down the field with the ball. Amelia bent her knees and readied herself to make a save. She slid on the turf as the forward kicked her in the head. She was able to get up and kept playing. Later Amelia was diagnosed with a concussion. Time passed and she wasn't getting any better. Her mother said she wasn't the child they knew. It was as if she had lost her spirit. She struggled in school and suffered many neck aches and headaches.

Her parents brought her in to see Sherrie, who discovered that Amelia had an undiagnosed vestibular problem, which is a balance disturbance or dizziness. Most people think concussions only affect male athletes in football and other rough sports, but Sherri says, "One of the highest incidences of undiagnosed concussion is in women's soccer."

One treatment Sherrie and her physical therapist, Ann McNamara, have used is a cutting-edge treatment in a flume. This is a small pool that simulates zero gravity and helps the athlete regain balance. Amelia's vestibular problems caused her eyes to not track properly, resulting in eyestrain and severe headaches, which led to poor schoolwork. Sherrie also uses osteopathic manipulative treatment (OMT) to treat Amelia's headaches and heal the musculoskeletal system. The athlete lies on the examining table while the doctor pushes on the body's tender points (places where pressure is felt). Each tender point has a corresponding spot on the body. When that spot is manipulated, often the tender point disappears. Sometimes this takes numerous treatments.

Amelia is getting better, and Sherrie says the family has been transformed by all they've learned about concussion treatment.

A large part of osteopathic medical training is a focus on the whole person, making it very multifaceted. For example many of the symptoms of a concussion—moodiness, headache, and depression—appear in everyday teens without a concussion. It's up to Sherrie and her team to focus in on what's really happening.

An important part of the standardized concussion management is working closely with the schools. The Boulder school district recently passed a program to get kids back to school earlier after a concussion.

Often this means adjusting for the symptoms of light and noise sensitivity. Teachers can let the students take a test in a quiet room or give them more time to complete it. Resting in the nurse's office also helps. Sherrie strives to get the student athlete back to a normal routine, helping to minimize the concussion symptom of depression. Sherrie is really proud of these new programs. "The parents literally give us a hug after their appointments because they think their kids won't recover but then their kids do get better and we get them back on track."

She also is passionate about helping students in the performing arts, such as dance and music. She works with the Performing Arts Medical Association to make sure these athletes are supported since they often fall outside the varsity athletic programs at high schools.

Sherrie looks out for female athletes who work too hard at their sport, leading to the female athlete triad. The triad occurs when the athlete stops getting a period, which depletes estrogen and opens her up to stress fractures and other injuries. The third component is the athlete's need for more and better nutrition. The long hours spent on training and competitions deplete the calories the athletes consumed and they can't maintain a healthy body weight. Sherrie studies their training and educates them on how to maintain a strong energy balance.

In thinking about advice to a young woman interested in medicine, she says, "Medicine has changed, it is no longer a way to make a lot of money." She said it is important to take the negative people out of your life and surround yourself with "truth tellers, those who can tell you when you're not acting like yourself or losing yourself. You can be a girl and still be in the male dominated sports medicine field."

LEARN MORE

Concussion Management in Boulder, Colorado, www.youtube.com/watch?v=0PEvncAA3CY&feature=youtu.be

Fourth Down and Inches: Concussions and Football's Make-or-Break Moment by Carla Killough McClafferty (Carolrhoda Books, 2013)

Sports Medicine Research by Gail B. Stewart (Reference Point Press, 2013)

Acknowledgments

I have always been an admirer of people who fight insurmountable odds. After researching and "living" with these brave medical women for a year or so, I am even more impressed. Their courage and persistence astounds me.

There are many people along the way who have helped me through this process. I first learned about this opportunity from Jodell Sadler (a former classmate in the master of fine arts in writing for children and young adults at Hamline University), now a literary agent at the Jill Corcoran Literary Agency. Thanks for helping me through the proposal and acquisition process and answering all my questions. And agent Karen Grencik of Red Fox Literary and Claire Rudolf Murphy my faculty advisor at Hamline, who believed in my early nonfiction work, thank you.

Many thanks to editor Lisa Reardon for supporting this book, pushing me to dig deeper in the introductions, and especially her patience as I worked through the photo permissions process for the first time. And thank you to project editor Lindsey Schauer, designer Sarah Olson, freelance copyeditor Julia Loy, and the rest of the team at Chicago Review Press.

The photograph research process was made infinitely easier because of Maureen and Aliza McKamey. Thank you to Michael Claussen at the Frontier Nursing Service for allowing me the use of two photos of Mary Breckinridge. And thank you to Pat McKay at the Rochester Hills Museum at Van Hoosen Farm for the use of Dr. Bertha Van Hoosen photographs.

Aimée Bissonette, Annette Spencer, Ann Matzke, Ann Quiring, and Leigh Klobucar, thank you for your guidance and friendship.

The Muskrats, my Tuesday evening writing group led by Jane Resh Thomas, what would I have done without you? Susan Brousseau, Katy Goodell, Laurie Johnson, Kristin Gallagher, Caren Stelson, and Patrick Brown, you patiently listened to each medical woman's story and provided me with praise, questions, and a critical eye.

Thanks to Meg Richard for connecting me with Dr. Sherrie Ballantine-Talmadge. To each of the modern-day medical women, Catherine Hamlin, Edna Adan Ismail, Anne Brooks, Kathy Magliato, Bonnie Mason, Adele Levine, and Sherrie Ballantine-Talmadge, thank you for allowing me to tell your fascinating stories. Each one of you was gracious with your time, which I know is a precious commodity. And to Gina Routh for writing the introduction about her recent journey through medicine. She provided a perspective geared toward future medical women.

To my extended family and my mom, Cynthia McGarvey, thanks for asking about the book and supporting me in every way.

To my sons, Ryan and Robbie, thanks for editing early drafts, providing encouragement, and brainstorming titles. To my daughter, Kristen, the future physician, thank you for the connections to the medical community, your ingenious wordsmithing, and guiding me through hours of technological difficulties. I am a lucky mother!

To my husband, Rob, for putting up with my three messy home offices, devising intriguing titles, and, most of all, listening to my writing disappointments and successes. Thank you for years of love and support—couldn't have done it without you!

Notes

All interviews cited were conducted by the author.

FOREWORD

As of this writing, Gina Routh was in her last year of medical school at Des Moines University. In May 2016 she graduated and became Dr. Gina Routh, D.O. (doctor of osteopathic medicine). She began an internal medicine residency in July 2016 at the University of Iowa, Des Moines.

INTRODUCTION

"Go Tomorrow to the Hospital": "Pioneers in the Face of Adversity: 'The Mob of '69,'' Doctor or Doctress?, Drexel University College of Medicine Legacy Center, http://doctordoctress.org/islandora/object/islandora%3A1347.

"When the ladies entered the": "Pioneers in the Face of Adversity."

"When we turned up at the clinic": "Current Topics of the Town."

PART I: THE BOLD PIONEERS

"For what is done or": Elizabeth Blackwell and Emily Blackwell, "Medicine as a Profession for Women," (lecture series, Clinton Hall, New York, 1860).

"You know very well that": Ruth J. Abram, ed., *Send Us a Lady Physician: Women Doctors in America, 1835–1920* (New York: W. W. Norton, 1985), 96.

FLORENCE NIGHTINGALE (1820–1910): VICTORIAN RULE BREAKER

"I think one's feelings waste": Edward Cook, *A Short Life of Florence Nightingale* (New York: MacMillan, 1931), 94.

"for something worth doing instead": Gena K. Gorrell, *Heart and Soul: The Story of Florence Nightingale* (Plattsburgh, NY: Tundra Books of Northern New York, 2000), 17.
"God spoke to me and": Mark Bostridge, *Florence Nightingale: The Making of an Icon* (New York: Farrar, Straus and Giroux, 2008), 54.
"Why cannot a woman follow": Gillian Gill, *Nightingales: The Extraordinary Upbringing and Curious Life of Miss Florence Nightingale* (Random House, 2004), 199.
"I hope in a few days": Barbara Montgomery Dossey, *Florence Nightingale: Mystic, Visionary, Healer* (Springhouse, PA: Springhouse, 2000), 126.
"It is a face not easily": Cook, *A Short Life*, 134.
"to affect thro' the Eyes": Julie Rehmeyer, "Florence Nightingale: The Passionate Statistician," *Science News*, November 26, 2008.
"statistics . . . is the most important": Dossey, *Florence Nightingale*, 227.

ELIZABETH BLACKWELL (1821–1910): MEDICAL PIONEER

"I do not wish to": Elizabeth Blackwell to Anne Isabella Milbanke Byron, 4 March 1851, Blackwell family papers.
"You are fond of study": Elizabeth Blackwell, *Pioneer Work in Opening the Medical Profession to Women: Autobiographical Sketches* (London: Longmans, Green, 1895), 27.
"I felt that I was": Blackwell, *Pioneer Work*, 33.
"To Elizabeth Blackwell, Philadelphia": Dorothy Clarke Wilson, *Lone Woman: The Story of Elizabeth Blackwell, the First Woman Doctor*, (Boston: Little, Brown, 1970), 152.
"For three weeks I lay": Blackwell, *Pioneer Work*, 155.
"food, air, sleep, exert a": Wilson, *Lone Woman*, 284.
"These malicious stories are painful": Blackwell, *Pioneer Work*, 197.
"Who will ever guess the": Blackwell, *Pioneer Work*, 198.
"One who never turned": Tristan Boyer Binns, *Elizabeth Blackwell: First Woman Physician* (New York: Franklin Watts, 2005), 97.

CLARA BARTON (1821–1912): BOLD ANGEL

"I may be compelled to": Elizabeth Brown Pryor, *Clara Barton: Professional Angel* (Philadelphia: University of Pennsylvania Press, 1987), 80.
"anywhere between the bullet and": Pryor, *Clara Barton*, 93.
"At 10 o'clock Sunday our": Clara Barton Papers, Speeches and Writings File, 1849–1947, war lectures, Library of Congress, 13.
"how we put socks and": Clara Barton Papers, 19.
"Army crackers put into knapsacks": Clara Barton Papers, 39.
"I must not rust much": Pryor, *Clara Barton*, 70.
"I am naturally businesslike and": Pryor, *Clara Barton*, 71.

"music I sleep by": Pryor, *Clara Barton*, 79.
"Angel of the Battlefield": Pryor, *Clara Barton*, 99.

MARIE ZAKRZEWSKA (1829–1902): WOMAN'S SPIRITED ALLY

"I prefer to be remembered": *Marie Elizabeth Zakrzewska: A Memoir* (Boston: New England Hospital for Women and Children, 1903), 7.
"little blind doctor": Marie Elizabeth Zakrzewska, *A Woman's Quest: The Life of Marie E. Zakrzewska, M.D.* (New York: D. Appleton, 1924), 17.
"I learned all of life": *Marie Elizabeth Zakrzewska*, 10.
"I soon ceased to be": Zakrzewska, *Woman's Quest*, 65.
"heart rich in faith and": *Marie Elizabeth Zakrzewska*, 11.
"I then went to the": Zakrzewska, *Woman's Quest*, 91.
"From this call . . . I date": Marie Elizabeth Zakrzewska, *A Practical Illustration of "Woman's Right to Labor"; or, A Letter from Marie E. Zakrzewska, M.D., Late of Berlin, Prussia* (Caroline H. Dall, 1860; repr. New York: Leopold Classic Library, 2015), 76.
"Marie Zakrzewska, a German about": Elizabeth Blackwell, *Pioneer Work in Opening the Medical Profession to Women: Autobiographical Sketches* (London: Longmans, Green, 1895), 201.
"I finally gave up looking": Zakrzewska, *Practical Illustration*, 89.
"new-fangled European notions": Zakrzewska, *Woman's Quest*, 251.
"The excess of work was": *Marie Elizabeth Zakrzewska*, 17.
"When I looked into that": *Marie Elizabeth Zakrzewska*, 21.
"The ocean is blue like": *Marie Elizabeth Zakrzewska*, 23.
"We stood no longer alone": Zakrzewska, *Woman's Quest*, 358.

REBECCA LEE CRUMPLER (1831–1895) AND REBECCA COLE (1846–1922): THE FIRST AFRICAN AMERICAN WOMEN PHYSICIANS

"My chief desire in presenting": Rebecca Lee Crumpler, *A Book of Medical Discourses in Two Parts*, (Boston: Cashman, Keating, 1895), 119.
"must satisfy the Faculty that": *Eleventh Annual Report of the New-England Female Medical College* (Boston: Trustees of the New-England Female Medical College, 1860), 6, https://open.bu.edu/bitstream/handle/2144/16154/NEFMC1860_web.pdf?sequence=2&isAllowed=y.
"It is certainly very appropriate": "Medical Practice by Women," *Daily Evening Traveller*, Boston Evening Traveller, March 9, 1864.
"To Mothers, Nurses, and all who": Crumpler, *Book of Medical Discourses*, dedication page.
"It may be well to state": Crumpler, *Book of Medical Discourses*, 2.
"proper field for real missionary": Crumpler, *Book of Medical Discourses*, 2.
"During my stay there nearly": Crumpler, *Book of Medical Discourses*, 2.
"with renewed vigor, practicing outside": Crumpler, *Book of Medical Discourses*, 2.

"They seem to forget that": Crumpler, *Book of Medical Discourses*, 4.
"Washing is the name given": Crumpler, *Book of Medical Discourses*, 14.
"This post was filled by": "Dr. Rebecca J. Cole," Changing the Face of Medicine, US Library of Medicine, www.nlm.nih.gov/changingthe faceofmedicine/physicians/biography_66.html.
"all the qualities essential to": "Dr. Rebecca J. Cole."

MARY EDWARDS WALKER (1832–1919): GUTSY SURGEON IN PANTS

"I am the original new": "Dr. Mary Edwards Walker," Changing the Face of Medicine, US Library of Medicine, www.nlm.nih.gov/changingthe faceofmedicine/physicians/biography_325.html.
"Dr. Mary E. Walker be": Mercedes Graf, *A Woman of Honor: Dr. Mary E. Walker and the Civil War* (Gettysburg, PA: Thomas Publications, 2001), 32.
"A brilliant idea had commenced": Graf, *Woman of Honor*, 32.
"Her reputation is unsullied, and": Graf, *Woman of Honor*, 34.
"I again offer my services": Graf, *Woman of Honor*, 65.
"weary soul in a weary frame": Nineteenth Century Dress Reform in Pictures, http://dressreform.tripod.com.
"Woman will never hold her": Nineteenth Century Dress Reform.
"We have no trailing dress": "Dr. Mary Walker," Nebraska State Historical Society, www.nebraskahistory.org/publish/publicat/timeline/walker-dr-mary.htm.
"has rendered valuable service to": "Walker, Dr., Mary E.," Congressional Medal of Honor Society, www.cmohs.org/recipient-detail/1428/walker-dr-mary-e.php.

PART II: MEDICAL WOMEN MAKING HEADWAY

"A measure of victory has": Elizabeth Kenny, *And They Shall Walk* (New York: Dodd, Mead, 1943), 272.
"A century ago the strongest": Bertha Van Hoosen, *Petticoat Surgeon* (Chicago: Pellegrini and Cudahy, 1947), 213.

BERTHA VAN HOOSEN (1863–1952): UNSTOPPABLE PETTICOAT SURGEON

"Perhaps I was different": Bertha Van Hoosen, *Petticoat Surgeon* (Chicago: Pellegrini and Cudahy, 1947), 69.
"The belly of the hog": Van Hoosen, *Petticoat Surgeon*, 26.
"I am not only going": Van Hoosen, *Petticoat Surgeon*, 57.
"My fear was transformed into": Van Hoosen, *Petticoat Surgeon*, 108.
"When I was born, the": Maureen Thalmann, *Petticoat Surgeon: The Extraordinary Life of Dr. Bertha Van Hoosen* (Oakland, MI: In the Fullness of Time, 2014), 109.

SUSAN LA FLESCHE PICOTTE (1865–1915): A BRIDGE BETWEEN WORLDS

"It has always been a": Valerie Sherer Mathes, *Susan La Flesche Picotte, M.D.: Nineteenth-Century Physician and Reformer: Great Plains Quarterly* (summer 1993), 175.
"It was a weary toilsome": Benson Tong, *Susan La Flesche Picotte, M.D.: Omaha Leader and Reformer* (Norman: University of Oklahoma Press, 1999), 26.
"Indians are only beginning": Tong, *Susan La Flesche Picotte*, 62.
"I can do a great": Edward E. Hale, *Lend a Hand: A Journal of Organized Philanthropy, 1886* (London: Forgotten Books, 2017), 1:500.
"interesting to get all the": Tong, *Susan La Flesche Picotte*, 73.
"courage, constancy, and ability": Tong, *Susan La Flesche Picotte*, 84.
"not a child in bed": Tong, *Susan La Flesche Picotte*, 90.
"a good influence with the": Tong, *Susan La Flesche Picotte*, 89.
"My office hours are any": Tong, *Susan La Flesche Picotte*, 93.
"This summer taught me a": Mathes, *Great Plains Quarterly*, 179.

ELIZABETH KENNY (1880–1952): DOGGED NURSE FROM THE OUTBACK

"It is better to be": Victor Cohn, *Sister Kenny: The Woman Who Challenged the Doctors* (Minneapolis: University of Minnesota Press, 1975), 33.
"wild one": Wade Alexander, *Sister Elizabeth Kenny: Maverick Heroine of the Polio Treatment Controversy* (Queensland, Australia: Central Queensland University Press, 2003), 18.
"Infantile Paralysis": Elizabeth Kenny, *And They Shall Walk* (New York: Dodd, Mead, 1943), 23.
"I knew the relaxing power": Kenny, *And They Shall Walk*, 24.
"I want them rags that": Kenny, *And They Shall Walk*, 24.
"The way before you is": Kenny, *And They Shall Walk*, 30.
"If I have only six": Cohn, *Sister Kenny*, 64.
"Although my special life's work": Kenny, *And They Shall Walk*, 74.
"Although I was well into": Kenny, *And They Shall Walk*, 200.
"Though we did not know": Kenny, *And They Shall Walk*, 216.
"She wasn't a quitter": Alexander, *Sister Elizabeth Kenny*, 119.
"There are power in her": Cohn, *Sister Kenny*, 165.

MARY CARSON BRECKINRIDGE (1881–1965): MOUNTAINEER NURSE ON HORSEBACK

"Winter had set in early": Mary Breckinridge, *Wide Neighborhoods: A Story of the Frontier Nursing Service* (Lexington: University Press of Kentucky, 1952), 178.
"Her eyes were luminous": Breckinridge, *Wide Neighborhoods*, 57.

"The more we seek to": "Mary Breckinridge," Frontier Nursing Service, https://frontiernursing.org/History/MaryBreckinridge.shtm.
"Well, the Duvauchelle family had": Breckinridge, *Wide Neighborhoods*, 84.
"They came in carload lots": Breckinridge, *Wide Neighborhoods*, 84.
"I rode down Muncy Creek": Breckinridge, *Wide Neighborhoods*, 121.
"riding sideways, on the rump": Breckinridge, *Wide Neighborhoods*, 245.
"We knew the minute we": Breckinridge, *Wide Neighborhoods*, 246.

HELEN TAUSSIG (1898–1986): FROM BLUE TO A LOVELY SHADE OF PINK

"A good research doctor has": Lynn Gilbert and Gaylen Moore, *Particular Passions: Talks with Women Who Have Shaped Our Times* (New York: Clarkson N. Potter, 1981), 57.
"Who is going to be": Joyce Baldwin, *To Heal the Heart of a Child: Helen Taussig, M.D.* (New York: Walker, 1992), 23.
"contaminate the male students": Baldwin, *To Heal the Heart*, 24.
"That which is a disappointment": Gilbert and Moore, *Particular Passions*, 53.
"Helen, for a woman, recognition": Ellen S. More, *Restoring the Balance: Women Physicians and the Profession of Medicine, 1850–1995* (Cambridge, MA: Harvard University Press, 1999), 178.
"crossword puzzles of Harriet Lane": Baldwin, *To Heal the Heart*, 47.
"I stand in awe and": Baldwin, *To Heal the Heart*, 53.
"When I saw Eileen for": "That First Operation," Blue Baby Exhibit, www.medicalarchives.jhmi.edu/firstor.htm.
"The boy's a lovely color": "That First Operation."
"Over the years": Gilbert and Moore, *Particular Passions*, 56.
"Physician, physiologist and embryologist": Lyndon B. Johnson, "Remarks at the Presentation of the 1964 Presidential Medal of Freedom Awards," September 14, 1964, American Presidency Project, www.presidency.ucsb.edu/ws/?pid=26496.

VIRGINIA APGAR (1909–1974): THE APGAR SCORE

"Nobody, but nobody, is going": Virginia Apgar Papers, Profiles in Science, US National Library of Medicine, https://profiles.nlm.nih.gov/CP/.
"Oh, I didn't know Apgar": "Obstetric Anesthesia and a Scorecard for Newborns, 1949–1958," Virginia Apgar Papers, Profiles in Science, US National Library of Medicine, https://profiles.nlm.nih.gov/ps/retrieve/Narrative/CP/p-nid/181.
"lifted birth defects from a": L. Stanley James, "Fond Memories of Virginia Apgar," *Journal of Pediatrics* 55, no. 1 (1975): 1–4.
"Be good to your baby": Melinda Beck, "How's Your Baby? Recalling the Apgar Score's Namesake," *Wall Street Journal*, May 26, 2009.

"Heavens, no. Never!": Laurie Scrivener and J. Suzanne Barnes, *A Biographical Dictionary of Women Healers: Midwives, Nurses, and Physicians* (Westport, CT: Oryx, 2002), 7.
"it was not what she": James, "Fond Memories," 1–4.
"tires never wore out because": James, "Fond Memories," 1–4.
"With her, life was exciting": "Second Career: The National Foundation–March of Dimes, 1959–1974," Virginia Apgar Papers, Profiles in Science, US National Library of Medicine, https://profiles.nlm.nih.gov/ps/retrieve/Narrative/CP/p-nid/182.

PART III: AND TODAY STILL FIGHTING

"True, women's hearts tend to": Kathy E. Magliato, *Heart Matters: A Memoir of a Female Heart Surgeon* (New York: Three Rivers, 2010), 20.
"I saw it coming": Carole Cadwalladr, "Nepal Earthquake: British Doctor Saved 23 Lives After Everest Avalanche," *Guardian*, May 9, 2015, www.theguardian.com/world/2015/may/09/nepal-earthquake-british-doctor-everest-avalanche-rachel-tullet.
"She was an absolute superwoman": Cadwalladr, "Nepal Earthquake."

CATHERINE HAMLIN (B. 1924): THE FISTULA PILGRIMS

"We're giving a young, beautiful": "Devoted Healer of Injured Women in Ethiopia," *Ethiopian Times*, February 18, 2012, https://theethiopiantimes.wordpress.com/2012/02/18/devoted-healer-of-injured-women-in-africa/.
"Reg said, 'Don't worry, Cath'": Catherine Hamlin, *The Hospital by the River: A Story of Hope* (Oxford: Monarch Books, 2004), 5.
"God will reward you for": Hamlin, *Hospital by the River*, 86.
"There was never any question": Hamlin, *Hospital by the River*, 115.
"I listened and had a": Hamlin, *Hospital by the River*, 138.
"God's clear guidance": Hamlin, *Hospital by the River*, 149.
"Oh, Pippa, you may have": Hamlin, *Hospital by the River*, 63.
"Reg and I, alone, cut": Hamlin, *Hospital by the River*, 166.
"On this occasion I was": Hamlin, *Hospital by the River*, 245.
"We have to eradicate Ethiopia": Nicholas Kristof, "At 90, This Doctor Is Still Calling," *New York Times*, February 5, 2014, www.nytimes.com/2014/02/06/opinion/kristof-at-90-this-doctor-is-still-calling.html.

EDNA ADAN ISMAIL (B. 1937): THE DUMP THAT BECAME A HOSPITAL

"Don't ever underestimate the capacity": "Who We Are," Edna Adan Hospital Foundation, http://ednahospitalfoundation.org/about/who-we-are/.
"I was not consulted, I": Nicholas Kristof and Sheryl WuDunn, *Half the Sky: Turning Oppression into Opportunity for Women Worldwide* (New York: Vintage Books, 2010), 123.

"was compassion and the value": Katy Migiro, "Edna Adan Ismail Puts Compassion at the Heart of an African Hospital," *Christian Science Monitor,* December 5, 2013, www.csmonitor.com/World/Making-a-difference/Change-Agent/2013/1205/Edna-Adan-Ismail-puts-compassion-at-the-heart-of-an-African-hospital.

"but what are you going": "Somaliland's Maternal Health Pioneer, Edna Adan Ismail," *The Stream*, YouTube video, January 20, 2014, www.youtube.com/watch?v=9ReIIJHH9qI.

"You're with women at a": "Somaliland's Maternal Health Pioneer, Edna Adan Ismail."

"what it has become gives": Teri Whitcraft, "Half the Sky: Edna Adan's Crusade for Women's Health," *Good Morning America* blog, October 1, 2012, http://abcnews.go.com/blogs/health/2012/10/01/how-edna-adan-built-somalias-first-maternity-hospital/.

"was a sore, an ulcer": Whitcraft, "Half the Sky."

"Education is one of the": "Edna Adan Ismail—If We Can Train Midwives in Somaliland, Everyone Can!," TEDxRC2 Geneva, October 10, 2011, YouTube video, accessed December 10, 2015, www.youtube.com/watch?v=hxJ8LELZCjo.

"Don't just take it lying": Migiro, "Edna Adan Ismail Puts Compassion at the Heart."

"The world needs midwives who": "Breakfast Briefing on 'State of the World's Midwifery 2011'—World Health Assembly," Partnership for Maternal, Newborn and Child Health, May 17, 2011, www.who.int/pmnch/media/press/2011/20110517_breakfast_at_wha/en/.

"FGM has no place as": "Who We Are."

"This little hospital": Whitcraft, "Half the Sky."

ANNE BROOKS (B. 1939): SISTER DOCTOR WITH ATTITUDE

"I have come to believe": Unpublished writings of Dr. Sister Anne Brooks, sent as part of e-mail correspondence with Sister Anne Brooks, December 8, 2015.

"because I didn't want my": Helen Meldrum, *Characteristics of Compassion: Portraits of Exemplary Physicians* (Boston: Jones and Bartlett, 2010), 36.

"This work is not for": Ace Collins, *Stories Behind Women of Extraordinary Faith* (Grand Rapids, MI: Zondervan, 2008), 110.

"I was looking for the": Bill Shaw, "Sister Anne Brooks, Doctor and Nun, Practices Without Preaching to the Poor," *People*, March 23, 1987, www.people.com/archive/sister-anne-brooks-doctor-and-nun-practices-without-preaching-to-the-poor-vol-27-no-12/.

"Even if you ARE white": Anne E. Brooks, "The Wounded Healer," *Humane Medicine*, October 1991, 291–296.

"She was in her early": Brooks, "Wounded Healer," 292.

"I'm not here to make": Shaw, "Sister Anne Brooks."

"This place has changed me": Shaw, "Sister Anne Brooks."
"Oh, Joe was going to": Meldrum, *Characteristics of Compassion*, 44.
"a much different connection because": Meldrum, *Characteristics of Compassion*, 46.
"Sometimes, I'll ask them if": Byron Pitts, "Mississippi Doctor a Saint with a Stethoscope," *CBS Evening News*, March 7, 2012, accessed December 10, 2015, www.cbsnews.com/news/mississippi-doctor-a-saint-with-a-stethoscope/.
"'Til I croak, I guess": Pitts, "Mississippi Doctor a Saint."
"We do what we can": Saul Gonzalez, "Mississippi Delta Health Care," *Religion and Ethics Weekly*, September 24, 2010, www.pbs.org/wnet/religionandethics/2010/09/24/september-24-2010-mississippi-delta-health-care/7073/.

JERRI NIELSEN (1952–2009): ICY COURAGE

"More and more as I": Jerri Nielsen and Maryanne Vollers, *Ice Bound: A Doctor's Incredible Battle for Survival at the South Pole* (New York: Hyperion, 2001), 206.
"I believe in geographic cures": Nielsen and Vollers, *Ice Bound*, 6.
"Camp 69. T. −22°F": "Doomed Expedition to the South Pole, 1912," Eyewitness to History, www.eyewitnesstohistory.com/scott.htm.
"I stepped out into the": Nielsen and Vollers, *Ice Bound*, 46.
"Feel the cold": Nielsen and Vollers, *Ice Bound*, 91.
"small, hard lump.": Nielsen and Vollers, *Ice Bound*, 144.
"Antarctica was a place so": Nielsen and Vollers, *Ice Bound*, 148.
"I need to know how": Nielsen and Vollers, *Ice Bound*, 282.
"people are loved for what": Nielsen and Vollers, *Ice Bound*, 190.

KATHY MAGLIATO (B. 1962): A PERSISTENT HEART

"My life's work has been": Kathy E. Magliato, *Heart Matters: A Memoir of a Female Heart Surgeon* (New York: Three Rivers, 2010), 247.
"Your parents give you two": Magliato, *Heart Matters*, 41.
"If you treat all your": Magliato, *Heart Matters*, 45.
"full-metal jacket.": Magliato, *Heart Matters*, 47.
"Hold the arm and pull.": Magliato, *Heart Matters*, 49.
"surgeon's knife or the chemist's": Peter Tyson, "The Hippocratic Oath Today," NOVA, March 27, 2001, www.pbs.org/wgbh/nova/body/hippocratictic-oath-today.html.
"In order to be not": Magliato, *Heart Matters*, 54.
"Grab the heart and hold": Magliato, *Heart Matters*, 2.
"If you have a goal": Kathy Magliato, speech at Women's Leadership Conference (Mount St. Mary's University, Los Angeles, CA, September 10, 2013).
"What if the recipient of": Magliato, *Heart Matters*, 176.

"My job, the way I": Kathy Magliato, phone interview, July 21, 2015.
"sometimes it's kind of": Magliato, interview.
"The operating room feels like": Magliato, interview.
"very privileged journey": Magliato, *Heart Matters*, 28.
"I'm a big believer in": Magliato, interview.
"I don't even get out": Magliato, interview.
"I'm a really good juggler": Magliato, interview.

BONNIE SIMPSON MASON (B. 1970): TAKING IT TO THE NTH DIMENSION

"It's a team effort": Bonnie Simpson Mason, phone interview, April 15, 2015.
"I want to be a physical": Mason, interview, April 15, 2015.
"The decision to be a": Mason, interview, April 15, 2015.
"energy of a positive African": Mason, interview, April 15, 2015.
"Unfortunately a 2.99 does not": Mason, interview, April 15, 2015.
"We have to ask for": Bonnie Simpson Mason, phone interview, October 14, 2015.
"Don't let a one-time experience": Mason, interview, April 15, 2015.
"Mastering orthopedic surgery requires more": Jennie McKee, "The Power of a Positive Role Model," *AAOS Now*, May 2008.
"Orthopedics was traumatic more from": Mason, interview, April 15, 2015.
"OK, well my mom did": Mason, interview, April 15, 2015.
"chance to be at the": Mason, interview, April 15, 2015.
"It felt like someone had" : Mason, interview, April 15, 2015.
"I'm a surgeon, and I": Mason, interview, April 15, 2015.
"If you read the psalms": Mason, interview, April 15, 2015.
"My parents were living examples": Mason, interview, April 15, 2015.
"She showed me that my": McKee, "Power of a Positive Role Model."
"infinite number of dimensions": Mason, interview, April 15, 2015.
"A higher level of trust": Mason, interview, April 15, 2015.
"You have to balance this": Mason, interview, October 14, 2015.
"I wanted to create pathways": "2015 AAOS Diversity Award," Sedgewick Productions1, YouTube video, February 10, 2015, www.youtube.com/watch?v=gRAML_XZe8A.
"Think about the areas that": Mason, interview, April 15, 2015.

ADELE LEVINE (B. 1970): A LEAP OF FAITH

"Regardless of a patient's true": Adele Levine, *Run, Don't Walk: The Curious and Chaotic Life of a Physical Therapist Inside Walter Reed Army Medical Center* (New York: Avery, 2014), 12.
"I always felt like a": Adele Levine, e-mail interview, June 2015.
"Physical therapy was in the": Levine, interview.
"If I didn't get immediately": Levine, *Run, Don't Walk*, 49.

"You could drop me on": Levine, interview.
"I remember the day I": Levine, interview.
"The cadaver lab was in": Levine, interview.
"It was so important to": Levine, *Run, Don't Walk*, 43.
"get smoked,": Levine, *Run, Don't Walk*, 228.
"We learned some surprising things": Levine, *Run, Don't Walk*, 232.
"My friends looked at the": Levine, *Run, Don't Walk*, 161.
"Alive Day": Levine, *Run, Don't Walk*, 76.
"I remember thinking how crazy": Levine, interview.
"I like physical therapy because": Levine, interview.

SHERRIE BALLANTINE-TALMADGE (B. 1977): BACK ON THE FIELD!

"Graduating from college and medical": Sherrie Ballantine-Talmadge, e-mail interview, June 10, 2015.
"Wow, that's perfect for me": Sherrie Ballantine-Talmadge, phone interview, June 19, 2015.
"The best gift my parents": Ballantine-Talmadge, interview, June 19, 2015.
"I wouldn't be who": Ballantine-Talmadge, interview, June 19, 2015.
"This was my life, it": Ballantine-Talmadge, interview, June 19, 2015.
"His pioneering spirit, medical expertise": SportsMed–Wheaton Orthopaedics Ltd., https://sportsmedltd.com/wheaton-orthopaedics/
"Sherrie, I'm just not around": Ballantine-Talmadge, interview, June 19, 2015.
"Wouldn't the kids be better": Ballantine-Talmadge, interview, June 19, 2015.
"Dr. Ballantine once described my": Meredith Finsand, e-mail interview, November 5, 2015.
"I have a passion for": Ballantine-Talmadge, interview, June 19, 2015.
"Making the decision to leave": Ballantine-Talmadge, interview, June 19, 2015.
"It was the right": Ballantine-Talmadge, interview, June 19, 2015.
"A concussion is an injury": *Concussion in Sports*, ACMS Information On . . . , American College of Sports Medicine, www.acsm.org/docs/brochures/concussion-in-sports.pdf.
"One of the highest incidences": Sherrie Ballantine-Talmadge, phone interview, December 15, 2015.
"The parents literally give us": Ballantine-Talmadge, interview, December 15, 2015.
"Medicine has changed, it is": Ballantine-Talmadge, interview, June 19, 2015.

Bibliography

Titles with asterisk are especially suitable for young readers.

BOOKS

*Abram, Ruth, J. ed. *Send Us a Lady Physician: Women Doctors in America, 1835–1920*. New York: W. W. Norton, 1985.

Achterberg, Jeanne. *Woman as Healer: A Panoramic Survey of the Healing Activities of Women from Prehistoric Times to the Present*. Boston: Shambhala, 1990.

Alexander, Wade. *Sister Elizabeth Kenny: Maverick Heroine of the Polio Treatment Controversy*. Queensland, Australia: Central Queensland University Press, 2003.

*Apel, Melanie Ann. *Virginia Apgar: Innovative Female Physician and Inventor of the Apgar Score*. New York: Rosen, 2004.

Apgar, Virginia, and Joan Beck. *Is My Baby All Right?* New York: Trident, 1973.

*Baldwin, Joyce. *To Heal the Heart of a Child: Helen Taussig, M.D.* New York: Walker, 1992.

Blackwell, Elizabeth. *Pioneer Work in Opening the Medical Profession to Women: Autobiographical Sketches*. London: Longmans, Green, 1895.

Bold, Julia. *The Excellent Doctor Blackwell: The Life of the First Woman Physician*. London: Thistle, 2013.

Breckinridge, Mary. *Wide Neighborhoods: A Story of the Frontier Nursing Service*. Lexington: University Press of Kentucky, 1952.

Carroll, Linda, and David Rosner. *The Concussion Crisis: Anatomy of a Silent Epidemic*. New York: Simon and Schuster, 2011.

Cohn, Victor. *Sister Kenny: The Woman Who Challenged the Doctors*. Minneapolis: University of Minnesota Press, 1975

Collins, Ace. *Stories Behind Women of Extraordinary Faith*. Grand Rapids, MI: Zondervan, 2008.

Cook, Edward. *A Short Life of Florence Nightingale*. New York: MacMillan, 1931.

*Cox, Clinton. *Black Stars: African American Healers*. New York: John Wiley & Sons, 2000.

*Crofford, Emily. *Healing Warrior: A Story About Sister Elizabeth Kenny*. Minneapolis: Carolrhoda Books, 1989.

Crumpler, Rebecca Lee. *A Book of Medical Discourses in Two Parts*. Boston: Cashman, Keating, 1895.

Ditchfield, Christin. *Clara Barton: Founder of the American Red Cross*. New York: Franklin Watts, 2004.

Dossey, Barbara Montgomery. *Florence Nightingale: Mystic, Visionary, Healer*. Springhouse, PA: Springhouse, 2000.

Duffy, John. *The Healers: A History of American Medicine*. Chicago: University of Illinois Press, 1979.

*Ferris, Jerri. *Native American Doctor: The Story of Susan La Flesche Picotte*. Minneapolis: Carolrhoda Books, 1991.

Gardner, Caroline. *Clever Country: Kentucky Mountain Trails*. New York: Fleming H. Revell, 1931.

*Garza, Hedda. *Women in Medicine: Women Then—Women Now*. New York: Franklin Watts, 1994.

Gilbert, Lynn, and Gaylen Moore. *Particular Passions: Talks with Women Who Have Shaped Our Times*. New York: Clarkson N. Potter, 1981.

Gill, Gillian. *Nightingales: The Extraordinary Upbringing and Curious Life of Miss Florence Nightingale*. New York: Random House Trade Paperbacks, 2004.

Goan, Melanie Beals. *Mary Breckinridge: The Frontier Nursing Service and Rural Health in Appalachia*. Chapel Hill: University of North Carolina Press, 2008.

Golden, Kristen, and Barbara Findlen. *Remarkable Women of the Twentieth Century: 100 Portraits of Achievement*. New York: Friedman/Fairfax, 1998.

*Gorrell, Gena. *Heart and Soul: The Story of Florence Nightingale*. Plattsburgh, NY: Tundra, Books of Northern New York, 2000.

*Graf, Mercedes. *A Woman of Honor: Dr. Mary E. Walker*. Gettysburg, PA: Thomas Publications, 2001.

Grant, Ted, and Sandy Carter. *Women in Medicine: Celebration of Their Work*. New York: Firefly Books, 2004.

Green, Norma Kidd. *Iron Eye's Family: The Children of Joseph La Flesche*. Lincoln, NE: Johnsen, 1969.

Hacker, Carlotta. *The Indomitable Lady Doctors*. Toronto: Clarke, Irwin, 1974.

Hale, Edward E. *Lend a Hand: A Journal of Organized Philanthropy, Vol. 1, 1886.* London: Forgotten Books, 2017.

Hamlin, Catherine. *The Hospital by the River: A Story of Hope.* Oxford: Monarch Books, 2004.

*Hammer, Roger A. *American Woman: Hidden in History, Forging the Future.* Golden Valley, MN: The Place in the Woods, 1993.

Hays, Elinor Rice. *Those Extraordinary Blackwells.* New York: Harcourt, Brace & World, 1967.

Hine, Darlene, and Kathleen Thompson. *A Shining Thread of Hope.* New York: Broadway Books, 1998.

*Hooks, Gwendolyn. *Tiny Stitches: The Life of Medical Pioneer Vivien Thomas.* New York: Lee and Low Books, 2016.

Hudson, Wade. *Book of Black Heroes: Scientists, Healers, and Inventors.* East Orange, New Jersey: Just Us Books, 2003.

*Hunter, Shaun. *Leaders in Medicine.* New York: Crabtree, 1999.

Janik, Erika. *Marketplace of the Marvelous: The Strange Origins of Modern Medicine.* Boston: Beacon, 2014.

*Joinson, Carla. *Civil War Doctor: The Story of Mary Walker.* Greensboro, NC: Morgan Reynolds, 2007.

Kenny, Elizabeth. *And They Shall Walk: The Life Story of Sister Elizabeth Kenny.* New York: Dodd, Mead, 1943.

*Ketchum, Liza. *Into a New Country: Eight Remarkable Women of the West.* New York: Little, Brown, 2000.

*LeClair, Mary K., Justin White, and Susan Keeter. *Three 19th Century Women Doctors: Elizabeth Blackwell, Mary Walker, and Sarah Loguen Fraser.* New York: Hofman, 2007.

Levin, Beatrice. *Women and Medicine.* Lanham, MD: Scarecrow, 2002.

Levine, Adele. *Run, Don't Walk: The Curious and Chaotic Life of a Physical Therapist Inside Walter Reed Army Medical Center.* New York: Avery, 2014.

Little, John. *Catherine's Gift: Stories of Hope from the Hospital by the River.* Oxford: Monarch Books, 2010.

*Luchetti, Cathy. *Medicine Women: The Story of Early-American Women Doctors.* New York: Crown, 1998.

Magliato, Kathy E . *Heart Matters: A Memoir of a Female Heart Surgeon.* New York: Three Rivers, 2010.

Marie Elizabeth Zakrzewska, a Memoir. Boston: New England Hospital for Women and Children, 1903. Harvard Library, https://iiif.lib.harvard.edu/manifests/view/drs:2575056$1i.

*McClafferty, Carla Killough. *Fourth Down and Inches: Concussions and Football's Make or Break Moment.* Minneapolis, MN: Carolrhoda Books, 2013.

McDonald, Lynn. *At First Hand.* London: Bloomsbury, 2010.

Meldrum, Helen. *Characteristics of Compassion Portraits of Exemplary Physicians.* Boston: Jones and Bartlett, 2010.

Morais, Herbert M. *The History of the Negro in Medicine.* New York: Publishers Company, 1967.

Morantz-Sanchez, Regina. *Sympathy and Science: Women Physicians in American Medicine.* Chapel Hill: University of North Carolina Press, 2000.

More, Ellen S. *Restoring the Balance: Women Physicians and the Profession of Medicine, 1850–1995.* Cambridge, MA: Harvard University Press, 1999.

More, Ellen S., Elizabeth Fee, and Manon Parry. *Women Physicians and the Cultures of Medicine.* Baltimore: Johns Hopkins University Press, 2009.

*Murphy, Jim. *Breakthrough! How Three People Saved "Blue Babies" and Changed Medicine Forever.* New York: Clarion Books, 2015.

*Newquist, H. P. *The Book of Blood: From Legends and Leeches to Vampires and Veins.* New York: Houghton Mifflin Books for Children, 2012.

*Newquist, H. P. *The Great Brain Book: An Inside Look at the Inside of Your Head.* New York: Scholastic Reference, 2004.

*Newquist, H. P. *The Human Body: The Story of How We Protect, Repair, and Make Ourselves Stronger.* New York: Viking, 2015.

Nielsen, Jerri, and Maryanne Vollers. *Ice Bound: A Doctor's Incredible Battle for Survival at the South Pole.* New York: Hyperion, 2001.

Nightingale, Florence. *Notes on Nursing.* New York: Dover Publications, 1969.

*Noyce, Pendred E. *Magnificent Minds: 16 Pioneering Women in Science & Medicine.* Boston: Tumblehome Learning, 2015.

Nuland, Sherwin. *Doctors: The Illustrated History of Medical Pioneers.* New York: Alfred A. Knopf, 1988.

Oates, Stephan B. *A Woman of Valor: Clara Barton and the Civil War.* New York: Free Press, 1994.

O'Malley, I. B. *Florence Nightingale, 1820–1856: A Study of Her Life Down to the End of the Crimean War.* London: Thornton Butterworth, 1931.

*Polacco, Patricia. *Clara and Davie: The True Story of Young Clara Barton, Founder of the American Red Cross.* New York: Scholastic, 2014.

Pryor, Elizabeth Brown. *Clara Barton: Professional Angel.* Philadelphia: University of Pennsylvania Press, 1987.

Quinn, Thomas A. *The Feminine Touch: Women in Osteopathic Medicine.* Kirksville, MO: Truman State University Press, 2011.

*Reef, Catherine. *Florence Nightingale: The Courageous Life of the Legendary Nurse.* New York: Clarion Books, 2017.

*Riley, Glenda, and Richard W. Etulain, eds. *By Grit and Grace: Eleven Women Who Shaped the American West.* Golden, CO: Fulcrum, 1997.

*Schatz, Kate. *Rad American Women A–Z.* San Francisco: City Lights Books, 2015.

Schiebinger, Londa. *The Mind Has No Sex? Women in the Origins of Modern Science.* Cambridge, MA: Harvard University Press, 1989.

Scrivener, Laurie, and J. Suzanne Barnes. *A Biographical Dictionary of Women Healers: Midwives, Nurses, and Physicians.* Westport, CT: Oryx, 2002.

Sicherman, Barbara, and Carol Hurd Green, eds. *Notable American Women: The Modern Period*. Cambridge, MA: Belknap Press of Harvard University Press, 1980.

*Somervill, Barbara. *Elizabeth Blackwell: America's First Female Doctor*. New York: Gareth Stevens, 2009.

Sterling, Dorothy, ed. *We Are Your Sisters: Black Women in the Nineteenth Century*. New York: W. W. Norton, 1984.

*Stewart, Gail B. *Sports Medicine Research*. San Diego, CA: Reference Point Press, 2013.

*Stille, Darlene R. *Extraordinary Women of Medicine*. New York: Children's Press, 1997.

*Stone, Tanya Lee. *Who Says Women Can't Be Doctors? The Story of Elizabeth Blackwell*. New York: Henry Holt, 2013.

Straus, Eugene W., and Alex Straus. *Medical Marvels: The 100 Greatest Advances in Medicine*. New York: Prometheus Books, 2006.

Stuart, Bonnye E. *More than Petticoats: Remarkable Minnesota Women*. Guilford, CT: TwoDot Press, 2004

*Swaby, Rachel. *Headstrong: 52 Women Who Changed Science—and the World*. New York: Broadway Books, 2015.

Thalmann, Maureen. *Petticoat Surgeon: The Extraordinary Life of Dr. Bertha Van Hoosen*. Oakland, MI: In the Fullness of Time, 2014.

Tong, Benson. *Susan La Flesche Picotte, M.D.: Omaha Indian Leader and Reformer*. Norman:, University of Oklahoma Press, 1999.

Tuchman, Arleen Marcia. *Science Has No Sex*. Chapel Hill: University of North Carolina Press, 2006.

*Van Hoosen, Bertha. *Petticoat Surgeon*. Chicago: Pellegrini and Cudahy, 1947.

*Walker, Dale L. *Mary Edwards Walker: Above and Beyond*. New York: A Tom Doherty Associates Book, 2005.

Walker, Mary. *HIT Essays on Women's Rights*. New York: American News Company, 1871.

*Walker, Sally M. *Frozen Secrets: Antarctica Revealed*. Minneapolis, MN: Carolrhoda Books, 2010

Walsh, Mary Roth. *"Doctors Wanted, No Women Need Apply": Sexual Barriers in the Medical Profession, 1835–1975*. New Haven, CT: Yale University Press, 1977.

*Wells, Rosemary. *Mary on Horseback: Three Mountain Stories*. New York: Dial Books for Young Readers, 1998.

Wilson, Dorothy Clarke. *Lone Woman: The Story of Elizabeth Blackwell, the First Woman Doctor*. Boston: Little, Brown, 1970.

Woodward, Helen Beal. *The Bold Women*. New York: Farrar, Straus and Young, 1953.

Zakrzewska, Marie Elizabeth. *A Practical Illustration of "Woman's Right to Labor"; or, A Letter from Marie E. Zakrzewska, M.D., Late of Berlin, Prussia.* Caroline H. Dall, 1860; repr. New York: Leopold Classic Library, 2015.

Zakrzewska, Marie Elizabeth. *A Woman's Quest: The Life of Marie E. Zakrzewska, M.D.* New York: D. Appleton, 1924.

INTERVIEWS

Ballantine-Talmadge, Sherrie. Telephone interviews, June 19 and December 15, 2015.

Cooper, Kiesha (assistant to Dr. Bonnie Simpson Mason). E-mail correspondence, July 27, August 27, October 8, October 15, November 20, 2015.

Finsand, Meredith. E-mail interview, November 5, 2015.

Herring, Cindy (assistant to Dr. Anne Brooks). E-mail correspondence, April 17, May 21, June 5, November 16, and December 8, 2015, and February 2, 2016.

Ismail, Edna Adan. E-mail correspondence, February 19, March 25, July 14, and December 8, 2015.

Levine, Adele. E-mail interviews, June 12 and November 22, 2015.

Magliato, Kathy. Telephone interview, July 21, 2015.

Mason, Bonnie Simpson. Telephone interviews, April 15 and October 14, 2015.

Montoya-Kaye, Maria (assistant to Dr. Kathy Magliato). E-mail correspondence, July 23, July 25, and December 8, 2015.

Routh, Gina. E-mail correspondence, September 23, November 8, November 12, 2015, January 24, 2016.

WEB LINKS

American Red Cross. www.redcross.org.

America Comes Alive. http://americacomesalive.com.

Antarctic Sun. http://antarcticsun.usap.gov.

Bertha Van Hoosen Exhibit, Rochester Hills, Michigan, ww3.rochesterhills.org/museum/exhibit1/vexmain1.htm.

Blackwell Family Papers, http://hdl.loc.gov/loc.mss/eadmss.ms998003.

Blue Baby Exhibit. www.medicalarchives.jhmi.edu/page1.htm.

Changing the Face of Medicine, National Library of Medicine. www.nlm.nih.gov/changingthefaceofmedicine.

Civil War Women (blog). http://civilwarwomenblog.com.

Clara Barton National Historic Site, US National Park Service. www.nps.gov/clba/learn/historyculture/index.htm.

Clara Barton Papers. Library of Congress. www.loc.gov/collections/clara-barton-papers/about-this-collection/.

Concussion in Sports (brochure). ACMS Info On . . . , American College of Sports Medicine. www.acsm.org/docs/brochures/concussion-in-sports.pdf.

Congressional Medal of Honor. www.cmohs.org.

The Connectory. http://theconnectory.org.

Courage Kenny Rehabilitation Institute history. www.allinahealth.org/Courage-Kenny-Rehabilitation-Institute/About-us/History.

Doctor or Doctress? Drexel University College of Medicine Legacy Center. http://doctordoctress.org.

"Doctor Van Hoosen, Surgical Mother." Chicago History Museum. http://blog.chicagohistory.org/index.php/2011/10/doctor-van-hoosen-surgical-mother.

"Dr. Mary Walker." Nebraska State Historical Society. www.nebraskahistory.org/publish/publicat/timeline/walker-dr-mary.htm.

Edna Adan Hospital Foundation. http://ednahospital.org.

"Engaging Girls in STEM." National Girls Collaborative Project. https://ngcproject.org/engaging-girls-in-stem.

FabFems. www.fabfems.org.

Florence Nightingale Museum. www.florence-nightingale.co.uk.

Frontier Nursing Service. https://frontiernursing.org.

Girls in Science Day. Des Moines University. www.dmu.edu/dose/tag/girls-in-science-day.

Hamlin Fistula Ethiopia web page. http://hamlin.org.au.

Hudec, Kate. "Map of the Human Heart." NOVA. www.pbs.org/wgbh/nova/body/map-human-heart.html.

National Girls Collaborative Project. https://ngcproject.org.

March of Dimes. www.marchofdimes.org.

National Science Foundation. www.nsf.gov.

National Women's History Museum. www.nwhm.org.

Nth Dimensions. www.nthdimensions.org.

Perry Initiative. http://perryinitiative.org.

Pitts, Byron. "Mississippi Doctor a Saint with a Stethoscope." *CBS Evening News* blog, March 7, 2012. Accessed December 10, 2015. www.cbsnews.com/news/mississippi-doctor-a-saint-with-a-stethoscope/.

Puckett, Susan. "10 Things to Know About the Mississippi Delta." CNN.com, May 15, 2014. www.cnn.com/2014/05/15/travel/mississippi-delta-10-things-bourdain/.

Richards, Laura. "Florence Nightingale: 1820–1910." Heritage History. www.heritage-history.com/index.php?c=academy&s=char-dir&f=nightingale.

Robert F. Scott journal. American Museum of Natural History. www.amnh.org/education/resources/rfl/web/antarctica/ej_scott.html.

Schierhorn, Carolyn. "Mississippi's First DO School Desperately Needed in Nation's Poorest State." The DO, April 20, 2012. https://thedo.osteopathic.org/2012/04/mississippis-first-do-school-desperately-needed-in-nations-poorest-state/.

"Sister Elizabeth Kenny: Leader in Physical Therapy: Overview." Minnesota History Center, Gale Family Library. http://libguides.mnhs.org/sisterkenny.

Sports Medicine Today. www.sportsmedtoday.com.

United States Antarctic Program. www.usap.gov.

"Want to Be a Doctor?" University of Washington Medical School, Youth web page. www.uwmedicine.org/education/md-program/admissions/youth/be-a-doctor.

Whitcraft, Teri. "Half the Sky: Edna Adan's Crusade for Women's Health." *Good Morning America* blog, October 1, 2012. http://abcnews.go.com/blogs/health/2012/10/01/how-edna-adan-built-somalias-first-maternity-hospital/.

Index

Page numbers in *italics* refer to pages with pictures.